Angelite

*Channelings from the Angels and
Saints About the World We Live In
and the World We Come From*

TAFFENY HICKS

ISBN: 978-0-69222-827-2

Cover design: West Kirkley
Interior design: Gary A. Rosenberg • www.thebookcouple.com
Photography: Marie Wallaker

Printed in the United States of America

Contents

Introduction

I have always known that we are not alone. Convincing other people to believe that has been my life's work. What if the Angels and Spirits of God didn't just speak to Adam and Eve and the members of the Bible? What if they could speak to us now? Would we listen and accept that our worlds exist together with only the veil of forgetfulness in between? My mother once asked me, "How do you know that when you ask God a question, he will answer, not Satan?" My reply was that I don't believe that when we cry out to God, the dark will answer us.

Fear of letting go of who we think we are is what keeps us ignorant of our true identity. My desire is that this book begins to dissolve your fears, quiet your mind, open your heart, and release your guilt. Only then, in the stillness, can we fully remember the voice of God.

Angelite has been many years in the making. I was directed in 2007 to begin writing the messages that the Divine helpers gave when they would appear to me. They instructed me to put them into a book so that as many people as possible could begin to read about their true identity. These messages of hope came through to me as I was going through many difficult trials and struggles in my own life. They brought me courage and joy and helped me to forgive myself and others.

Hard times come and go, but we do not experience them alone. We are all accompanied by an entourage of God's helpers: Angels and Spirits who support us, love us, and help us to pull through. I believe they are God's Divine Essence reaching down to touch every one of us and wake us from our spiritual slumber. Being lost is virtually impossible on this planet. Help is always a second away. *Angelite* was inspired, directed, and channeled by these Divine helpers.

For ten years, I channeled for a group of friends who became like family. This became known as our Spirit Group and really became our church. There are recordings in our library of messages from the Divine helpers. *Angelite* is just a small handful of the messages that I have channeled. They were handpicked by the Angel helpers. These messages were chosen as important for humankind to know now.

In the quiet hours of my life, the Divine helpers would come to me, and I would write and commune with them. I know they exist and that we have nothing to fear. Darkness will turn into light, but it has to begin in our minds. As we think, so we create. When our guilt and fear dissolve, punishment of any kind will cease—whether toward one another or ourselves.

I hope this book brings you understanding, knowledge, peace, and hope wherever the road takes you. Remember, the truth of your existence lies in your heart.

Blessings to you on your path to enlightenment.

"Angels can fly because they take themselves lightly . . ."
—GILBERT K. CHESTERTON

Angel Seth

Have No Fear of Endings

Greetings! I have come to bring good cheer. I have a message that may and should inspire the world. Though all seems lost, dark, and dreary, there will always be a light-filled ending. That was God's promise. It wasn't about just the rainbow and the flood. It was about the ending. The ending always seems to be dreaded and despaired by you humans. Why are you so scared of the end? It is because you equate all endings with "Judgment Day," Hell, and damnation. You are not really conscious of this. But if someone were to walk up and say, "Today is your last day," you would panic and expect the worst. I am here today to talk about endings—death as you call it. I guess you could call me the "Death Angel," and my appearance being described is not of much importance. What is important are endings, finalities, change. You get the picture.

Here is your first example: a mother bird lays many eggs. One day, they all begin to hatch. You happen to be one of them. Does anyone mourn, weep, or lament when the egg begins to break apart? Does the mother fear? No! And yet you will break out of your shell your whole life. At every stage of your life, you will have a shell to break through. This shell will be made up of many lessons, judgments, dogmas, programs, and no longer important priorities. So why does it seem so hard? Because this shell has protected, guarded, and kept you safe and supported you to its fullest. But guess what?

You can no longer fit into it! Would you like an example?

Picture this: you are twenty-nine years old. All of your life you have been to church "every time the door was open," as humans say. Now, you have found that this no longer fits you. You need something more, and it is not in that shell. It has served its purpose. You begin to break out and go hiking on Sunday mornings. You pray, meditate, and merge with Yahweh, or I AM. You are now finding another shell—a bigger shell. Is this wrong? Well, how can you say that a bird breaking from his shell is wrong? Didn't Yahweh create it? Of course! Then, why do you judge it and why are you scared? Maybe it is because you will find the truth of who you are! Your whole life you will always search for the "missing piece," and you will give up almost anything to find it. Do you know what this is? It is you! And when you find it, there Yahweh will be also.

Unfortunately, being in a human body, you will always desire to merge and be with I AM. You could become a saint, feed the hungry, walk with the dying, heal the sick, but guess what? At the end of the day, you will still feel one slot is empty. That is your merging. It is only natural for a form to somehow return to its true form. So, why do you think so many people seek? It is because they are so empty. They seek something greater than themselves.

Think of teenagers. They seek to be with the popular or someone who is "greater" in some form than they are—whether this be a teacher, student, parent, a drug, or alcohol. So then why don't we tell them seeking is okay? It is necessary to know what you are really seeking and to go toward the purest form; anything else will leave a bitter taste in the mouth.

Now, changing the subject, what becomes of the shell

when you come out of it? Do you curse it and kick it out of the nest? Really! You should give thanks and let it return back to the Earth. Here is another example: You decide to leave a particular church. You just don't seem to fit there anymore. Some things may have been said or done to create this. Do you become angry, fearful, and forever judge the dwelling of Yahweh or do you leave them, become thankful for the church or the shell, and what it has been for you? Do you allow it to return to Yahweh and do you go on to find another house or shell? Do you mourn for the broken shell? Do you see which one makes logical sense if you were a bird? So then why do you create karma with your anger, judgment, and sorrow?

Rise up, be thankful, release this shell, and go on to the next phase. Life is a progression. The ones who refuse to progress will sit around in their shells and never continue. Why do you do this? Would you mourn the birth of your child and sit around the afterbirth and cry? So, then, why do you mourn change? Change is really a birth in disguise of death. Here is where you gain your faith. Faith, I believe the Bible says is "believing in things that are unseen." Your future, your birth out of the shell, will call for you to have faith in tomorrow, because, guess what? Yahweh is tomorrow, and today, and all of the tomorrows. If Yahweh is already there, then why should you fear?

Have faith, little birdie. Faith that you are made with all the tools—wings, feathers, heart, and brain—that you should have. If Yahweh created you, then do what you were created for. Do not be afraid! Peace be upon all of you who have read this and all of you who will in the future. This is the word, untouched, unchanged, but in divine deed. Blessed are those who hunger, for they shall be filled. Amen.

> "[Angels] guide us to become spiritual people for
> the pleasure of it . . . because the spiritual life itself
> has a great deal of beauty and real satisfaction,
> even pleasure. And this is what the soul needs."
>
> —THOMAS MOORE

Angel Oriel
(Angel of the Rising Sun)

Find Your Key to
the Kingdom of Heaven

Good day! I am the angel of the rising Sun, here to do the deed and work that I've been created for. Today will be a summary of the events of the world. In the beginning there was One. All things came and were created by this One Source. The One began time, and everything seemed to trickle in to full existence. Yet, everything was created, but more was desired. Yes, the One desires. Where do you think desire comes from? So then you were created—created in the purest form, untouched by anything other than pure light.

One day, darkness crept in, and another path of creating was chosen. Now then you have the light and the dark to create. Falling to the Earth, Earth's time began to exist. It is from this point until the last desire to create that will spawn you to come down here. You cannot create something without a goal in mind. Just like you do not come down here without a goal, or as you call it, a purpose. You live your whole life finding out that you have one, then trying hard to get it done. Why do you do this? Because the purpose is the key back into your home.

Find the key, use it, and you can walk back into your heavenly home. Blessed are those who seek, for they shall find. All your life serve as you have never served before and seek as you have never sought before. Time on Earth grows short, and many will be down to the wire. Find your key into the kingdom. Hurry and don't be late. Amen.

"Since God often sends us inspirations by
means of His angels, we should frequently
return our aspirations to him by means
of the same messengers."
—FRANCIS DE SALES

Angel Jamarius

The Essence of Time

Time. "Time is of the essence," "I don't have much time," "Time is all I have." It seems that humans view time very differently. You view it as something that seems to be in control of you, and something that is out of your control. Well, you are wrong, incorrect, not right! Time is simply the one thing that you seem to possess. See, you have a plan, a clear direct plan or purpose here. It is up to you how long you choose to fulfill this plan. You also have windows or doors of opportunity to leave by your own choosing. Of course, these doors are created and offered.

Do you not realize that when you say, "I don't have enough time," or "There are not enough hours in the day" that you are creating it? Why do you think the world or Earth as a whole has sped up? It is only your perspective. And when things seem to be enough, globally, you will give yourself permission to slow down. Sometimes this equals disasters because you are causing a great shift. The Earth seems to respond mostly to man's conscious state. For instance: the more you take from the Earth with no thankfulness or respect, the more you are telling the Earth she is of no value.

The Earth is sort of a mother to you, so when you disrespect, you are disrespected back. She moves, grunts, and belches, causing earthquakes, landslides, and eruptions. Don't you get it? You all are running the planet by your every thought, deed, word, and action. It would be like millions of people with their hands on one big steering wheel. Now do you see? This might seem scary now! Do not be afraid—just realize what you are doing. When you want more, more, more and are not thankful for what you have, you are telling the Earth and God that they are not enough. When you do this, both retreat from you—not by their choice, but by yours.

When you are thankful and grateful, you are saying to the Earth and God that there will always be enough and so you have enough. This is the same with your time. Remember that God will give everyone enough time to fulfill his or her purpose. Why are you all so scared? If you fail, you will simply come back. You have enough time as you allow yourself and remember: A pure and thankful heart is always blessed beyond measure. So the next time you begin to utter nonsense about time, stop and be thankful. Declare there is enough and relax. All will be well. Blessed are those who thirst for they shall be given everlasting waters in which there is no end. Amen.

I see a vision of a garden. A beautiful angel stands with auburn hair, green gown, and wings of glory. About her head is a halo or lantern of light that she shines out so bright. A mere reflection of the God, the One, the I AM, within her. In her hand, she holds an hourglass, and according to man's asking and the granting of the I Am, she shifts the sand up and down so that we may continue. All should be grateful for her existence, as she has been created since the beginning of our time. Blessed are we for the keeper holds the very grains of sand between her blessed hands. Praise be to God for the granting of our existence. Amen.

> "And the angel said, 'I have learned that every man lives not through care of himself, but by love.'"
>
> —LEO TOLSTOY

Angel Julius

Be in the Now

Today is no ordinary day, nor is it a day to celebrate. The only difference in today is that you have it! Do you understand that now is the most important? Remember what Jesus taught: "Do not worry about your tomorrows for they will take care of themselves." Time on Earth is not like the time in Heaven. All things exist on one Unitarian plane. On Earth, things are high/low, good/bad, black/white, yesterday/tomorrow. This is why it is so hard for you to be in the now. Only through being in the now can you somehow link energies with the heavens and tap into universal light energies. Why do you think Jesus meditated? Jesus meditated to link or connect with what is real—the One Source.

Do not be dismayed when we Angels tell you to leave the past behind you. We are telling you to make peace and see it on a linear plane. Tomorrow will be a new day—something to laugh with and something to cry with. But when it comes, be in it, having made peace with your past and having no worry for your tomorrows. Do not do what so many people do.

They miss their whole life because of regretting or thinking about their past experiences and worrying about their future experiences. Woe to those who think they can escape the present moment, for the One will surely make them be present and learn how to connect.

What do you think that praying is about? Do not be foolish and think that time will escape you no matter what. But if you find yourself 100% truly present in the moment, you will have more bliss and peace than ever before. Remember, time on Earth is not like the time in Heaven. Come on . . . Plug in to the Real Source and find all of the things that will fill you up, all of the things that are everlasting, all of the things that have true meaning, all of the things that are without end. Amen.

Angels Julius and Ouronia

*Keep Your Eyes
on the True Source*

Too many people in this world are looking for earthly possessions to fill their souls. Why do you think the disasters have begun? Well, there are many reasons, but this one is because you, as a whole, have begun to shift your eyes off of the true existence. Possessions are temporary, not lasting nearly as long as you would have hoped for. Today there will be another disaster, one that is not seen or heard, but one that goes silent. This disaster is not feeling love. So many people are angry. So many people are frustrated. But Yahweh has allowed this energy because they were beginning to base their whole dependency and life, on worrying about the things of the Earth. Once that is taken from you, you have to walk on your own.

Many people still do not understand, so they curse Yahweh. They accuse any and all that would do this to them, but in reality, they have begun to bring disaster upon themselves. They still do not fall to their knees and connect, realizing their Source, but they wail and lament, expecting to be saved. Being truly saved is connecting with Yahweh. It will take time, but they will begin to understand. They will understand that their choices, decisions, thoughts, and false gods have aimed them at this state of discomfort. They do not seem to realize that this is a choice—a choice to see and realize and connect so that all will begin to be peaceful. This is a lesson for all. When you take your eyes off the true Source, the true Source will come searching for you and bring you home. In other words, it is like the shepherd finding the sheep that have gone astray. Think about it. The sheep have left the flock of the "true consciousness and connection" and have found another pasture that they think they want or is better for them. It can be devastating when they have to leave what they have chosen and be brought back into the flock of truth. Some of you say, "The truth hurts."

Well, sometimes it does because the façade is being shattered and a life shift occurs. Remember that all is well and will be well in the end. The truth will always set you free. Free from falseness, free from separation, free from what is not real. Do not worry, little one, the truth is Yahweh, and it will be here today, tomorrow, and in the future. It will not change nor will it end. Walk bravely knowing that if you walk in connection with truth and love, you will walk right into the pastures of the heavenly realm. This message is not about damnation or accusations for those of you who would want to see it this way. This is not about pointing the finger, but it is about love and truth. Understand that you are responsible for your actions and consequences. Many will read this and many will understand. Some of you will not. Continue reading this book.

We Angels of the most high will help you throughout. This message is for you. Why? Because God/Yahweh/Source/ Great Spirit/whatever you choose to call "It" loves you . . . Yes, you. Little ones, it is hard for you to understand the love of God. It is deeper than any ocean, cavern, or canyon: wider than the universe itself and brighter than any star. There is nothing that can separate you. You see that even if you turn your back and your eyes from Yahweh, the love remains. It's hard for the human mind to understand, but it is true.

In the next parts of the book, we will try to expand your views. Just relax, open your mind and your heart, and be blessed with the supernatural or spiritual understanding—for you have prayed for it. Bless you and your understanding. Amen.

"Let triumph the better angels of our nature."
—ABRAHAM LINCOLN

Angels Esteria, Zadkiel, and Archangel Michael

Find the Light Within Yourself First

What is doubt? It is the unbelief of what is or what could be. What is a belief? Having faith in something, someone, or an occurrence. What is faith? Knowing, believing. Why do we doubt and why are we not born with all the faith and belief we should have? These are questions many of you have asked yourself and God. What will be the point of today's message? Knowing when doubt is appropriate and when it is not. You see, having doubt in things that are not truths is perfection in action, but having doubts about something that is a truth is ignorance. Can one distinguish? Go within yourself. Ask God to show you the truth of what is. Then you will know. How many of you would ask a person instead of God? How many of you have done this already?

This is what the Bible means when it speaks of false prophets. What is a prophet? It is one who prophesies something. It could be a leader of the church, a politician, a doctor, lawyer, mate, etc. You see? Most people think of a false prophet as just one who will lead the church or religion. Not so. Now why do we tell you this? It is so that you will begin to let go or release man's truths and begin to see and hold on to God's truths. That is why you are to pray earnestly every day for guidance on your own. Do not sit back and allow another to lead you in all ways. Why do humans do this? You find someone who you see the light of God in and you follow him in most all things. Why do you do this? That would be like standing in a circle of mirrors and fleeing to the one who reflects the sun's light. Then to the next, then to the next.

Find the light within yourself first. Then you can see and understand it in others. Following others without seeking the truth on your own first is dangerous to your path. When you put so much focus on another, you begin to lose the value of yourself. Then all kinds of doubt seep in and you lose yourself. You see doubt should only be used appropriately. If you are to follow one's light or teachings, here are some rules: 1) Go within yourself first and find your own light, your value, and your truth in God. 2) Do not lose your total existence of who you are on this person. 3) Remember, we are all just channels for God. Some have a lot of static and some are pure and clear. All of your life, you will fight to keep out the static. Honor the guidance, and then pray on your own every day to God for your own channel or path. This is a lot to think about, but in the end, it will all make perfect sense to you.

Now, let's talk about your garden. Yes, your garden. What is it you are wishing to plant there? See the Earth or garden spot as a way of coming down here to create. This world within you is the world you will create. Many are lazy; they do not want to dig or till up the dirt. They would rather just do nothing. They do not usually stay down here for very long. And if they do, it will begin to get unbearable for them. Now, there are those who work and till and plow. They come down here as achievers ready to put their spiritual plan in action. Then, there are those unsure, but in the end, they begin to work on the Earth. Now that the garden is tilled, what will you plant? You have as many seeds and bags as you desire. There is no limit. Only you not using the bags limits you, but not God.

Will you plant seeds of love, charity, piousness, humility, and compassion? Or will you plant anger, hate, revenge, weakness, and the absence of love? This garden is yours to plant. Do you understand? Yours! Yes, the rains will come and the winds will blow, but you will learn to use this to your advantage. Remember in this garden, no matter what storm, animal, season, or weed destroys it, you can always start over and build another. See, this is where you humans get stuck. When you come out of a bad home life, a bad marriage, an abusive relationship, or an unpleasant job, you think it's over! You think you can never begin again! It does not matter if you sin or they sin when it comes to starting again; you all should.

Here is an example: a man, Paul, commits adultery several times and ends up divorced. The whole family suffers, and Paul becomes guilt ridden. He thinks it's over, he's guilty, he will always be accountable, and he is not worthy to begin planting again. Why? Does it make any sense to sit by your garden with all your tools and say you can't? Get up and try again. Heal thyself! That means let the Spirit of God that is within you connect with the God of all and mend and heal so that you are free of this.

Forgive yourself or you will never be free to plant again. When you do not forgive, you chain yourself up and cannot move. Why? Learn, love, forgive, and plant again. We urge you to come out of your prison. You see, God has not put you there; you did! There is no prison that can hold the light of God. So, we urge you to get up, plow, and plant your seeds of love, which will grow and yield you fruit that the whole world can eat right from your very garden. Amen.

> *"Who can know what tales are told*
> *in the whispers of an angel,*
> *Who can see what mighty deeds he*
> *does in the name of the Lord,*
> *What eye can see or mind conceive*
> *of how he sees this world,*
> *Dark and light is angel sight: the battle*
> *brave, and souls are saved.*
> *Demons flee when we're set free, and*
> *angels there attend."*
>
> —DENNIS CARLSON RAGSDALE

Angel Dionysus and Archangel Uriel

The Spirit Is the Light

Hello! A word about self-love. Many never understand this concept. First, we have to define what this self is. It is not the shell that you are within, it is not the mind that controls the shell, and it is not the heart that fuels the shell. It is the true self within you. Your Spirit. Mothers, fathers, it is important you teach your children how to find their true self. At first, they know, then the veil begins to fall and they forget. Then their true self leaves them little clues like the feeling of love, the feeling of charity, or the feeling of compassion. They like these feelings and so they migrate to the self from which these feelings come. Then and only then, after following the trail within, can they see and reach enlightenment.

Enlightenment for all can be very different even though we are all looking at our true self. Remember, the Spirit is the light reflected from the jewels of the mind and the heart, so that many will have a different color or perspective. You see, because theirs is a different color does not mean either of you are wrong. You just found your true self, a shade of a different color, but you are still the light. When you find this true self, stay there for a while. Just exist, be, merge, become one, and allow the healing of all lifetimes to begin. Why do you think Jesus meditated? Why do you think he had the capacity to heal completely? Why, because he knew who he was. He emerged daily and he held on to nothing other than the truth. He himself stayed in a state of being healed. Interesting?

You see, if you want to help heal others, heal yourself first. The more you heal or absorb the light, the more you can heal or reflect the light. Like a sponge, the more water or light you soak up, the more you can release. So now that we have found the healing place, or the place of the Spirit, you begin to love and honor your other parts. You love and honor your body, because it is a mirror that reflects Spirit's light. You love your mind because it is a mirror that reflects Spirit's light through thought, word, and deed. You love your heart because it reflects Spirit's light through emotion. You see, there is no room for selfishness. Amen.

*"Angels are sent to bring us messages
from God's heart."*
—CHARLES HUNTER

Angel Razchiel

We Are All Relations

Today, we will address the issues of black and white. Why were they made and why is everyone not one color? Well, why isn't everything in the world green? You see, Yahweh, creator, wanted to make everything unique and beautiful in all of its creation. Color is diversity, yet unity, because it is all made from the same Source. You see, everything came from one thought of the One. So then why do you judge things as good or bad when it is a color? Because you logically associate color with the goings-on of that particular matter.

Example: you don't eat meat in your refrigerator that has been there too long and turned dark and rancid. See, your body tells you by its color that it is bad or has spoiled. Yet, if you opened a container, and it had white fuzzy mold growing on it, you would associate it as bad. You see, the brain is a computer that wants to match things together. Yet it is not logical to assume humans, animals, or any other creature is bad because your brain has associated it with a previous experience—black cats, for example.

23

The point of today is to know the difference between when your brain is associating two things as one and when it is really protecting you and being logical. Racism is an evil that permeates all who are willing to allow it to come in. It is what teaches your mind or affirms to your mind that you are separate when in truth you are not. For instance, do you remember the color wheel lights used for Christmas trees? Each color has its own lens and as the circle rotates, the light shines through only one at a time. Now, they may have their own lens, but they all belong to one large wheel that shines the light through them. Do you understand? Color is color. Nothing less or more. Love your color and all the other colors in this world, knowing that Creator has made them all, and Creator will shine in them all. Amen.

I looked upon my beloved's face and they
upon mine. What would I see shining back
at me . . . Eternity. Eternity in full bloom.
Colors, many to see. Every creature, animal,
plant, and tree. Their reflection was within
me, a mural and revelation. For I have
realized that we are all relations! Amen.

> "We not only live among men, but there are airy
> hosts, blessed spectators, sympathetic lookers-on,
> that see and know and appreciate our thoughts
> and feelings and acts."
>
> —HENRY WARD BEECHER

Angel Hamiliel

Work with the Earth

Today we are going to talk about the sun. We are going to discuss how it influences our life and what it is really about. We are also going to discuss the evolutionary aspects of its age, origin, and what's next. Do you see the sun? Doesn't all food, water, and nutrients originate from its existence? Of course! The sun really is "the ruler" of the sky. According to man's past thoughts, you even considered it a god! You almost had it right. It is the ruler of this sky, but it is only made by God, used for God's divine plan, according to his will—one of God's masterpieces. You feel God's power, presence, warmth, and light in it. It is a small reminder of what the light and warmth of heaven is. Nothing more, nothing less. Now, how does this reflect your life? Well, of course, it has certain energies or plans God created for it, and it seems to be a constant for mankind.

Humans need things that are constant. They get very upset when things begin to change. This is why, when you are enduring major amounts of change and you are afraid, you should look up! Look up to the sun; look up to creation, heaven, the constant that never changes. Now, let's talk about planetary changes. These are changes that are coming that no one wishes to discuss. The world as we know it is old within its origins. The Earth has been through many, many catastrophic changes and will continue to change even more. How does this affect you humans, you ask? Well, you begin to adapt; you begin to change. Have you forgotten about evolution? If the sun feels hotter because the ozone is depleting, then don't you think that your skin will grow thicker and your melanin will adjust? Don't you think that trees will grow thicker leaves? See, whenever you have a slow shift as global warming, everything has a chance to evolve. It is when it is immediate or abrupt that it is difficult, and many exit the planet.

Now, do you understand that there will be both? You will evolve, yet there will be catastrophes to contend with. So is the law of the land. What do you think it means in the Bible when it discusses obeying the laws of the land? Not only was it talking about the laws of state, but also the laws of the Earth. What are the laws? Well, there are many, but I will give you four of them today:

1. Never take from without giving back.

2. Honor every living creature, plant, tree, stone, or matter, as if they are the very life and breath you breathe.

3. Never take more than you need.

4. Understand that everything has its place. Do not move it from its place, unless you are granted permission and unless appropriate.

You see, when you live in complete harmony with the Earth, the Earth will live in complete harmony with you. Mother Earth is a teacher. She is here, created and born, to give you your lessons. If you are not living within these lessons, then she will teach you how. Here are some examples:

- Hurricane Katrina.

- In the Bible, God told the Israelites not to take more manna than needed. They did not listen and the manna turned into worms by the next morning.

- Moses parted the Red Sea. He could part it because this was God's plan, and Moses obeyed the laws of the land. So, therefore, the sea granted his request and moved itself for safe passage.

- Moses struck the rock and brought forth water—again, obeying and living in harmony with the laws.

- Elisha multiplied the oil for the widow and her son. The oil multiplied itself. Elisha obeyed God, in harmony with the laws of the Earth, and the oil obeyed or granted his request.

Don't you see? This should be easy for you. Your homework is for one day to memorize the four laws. The second day, go forth and obey. Let's just see what happens. To God, be all the glory, for the message from the I AM will never cease. Truth will be heard, truth will be told, and truth will be taught to those who are willing and seeking a higher way. Not to be above anyone, but to be above one's own ego. Amen.

Angel Ambriel

Wholeness Comes from Using the Spiritual with the Physical

Times are slowly changing, and soon the whole world will be on the cusp of an evolution. An evolution that will surely take you into the next phase of God's plans. You see, in order to understand what is coming, you have to know what has been. This is why we are trying to explain to the world some of the things that they have not understood. When they are understood, then you will all be in understanding of what is coming. "Time flies when you're having fun." Do you know what that really means? It means when you are having joy, time really doesn't exist or matter. You come to a place of being. Existing in the being, you were supposed to. Everything begins to harmonize and balance. This is why when you laugh you begin to feel better. Laughter is like dumping a bottle full of light or Clorox into milky water. It starts getting rid of the things that are not good or prosperous for you. This is why the Bible says, "Laughter does the heart good like medicine."

Can you imagine existing in this state of being at least four days out of seven? What do you think would happen to your life? You would heal, love, forgive, become wise, but most of all, you would change the energy around you. That is what I came to talk to you about today. Prophecies are given to humans, so that they can understand where they are going. For example, some of the prophecies in the Bible have been devastating and horrific. Yet everyone believes that if a prophecy is given, it has to happen. We tell you where you are headed. For instance, if you are driving down a road and we see that it will be a dead end, then we will tell you. But you humans believe that it will inevitably happen. But if you decide to turn your car in another direction, then you will not hit the dead end! Do you understand? Only an average of 20% that happens in your life is fate. The rest is 80% free will. So, then, why do you give up and allow the dead ends to come? Because you do not have enough faith to "plug in" to your spiritual power Source and observe your options. Yes, I said, "FAITH!"

Faith is something that no human can see or touch, but it will grow within you if you feed it. It was placed there within you like a lighthouse to help you see your way. Many of you have "bulbs" that are not working or you just don't feel like repairing your lighthouse. No one other than you can fix it, although you will all have helpers when you decide to do this. Don't fret about all the work to get you there; just enjoy the repairs as they go. Why is it you humans can never see where you are at or where you are going? It is because you do not close your eyes. Yes, I said to close your eyes. When you do this your sleepy spiritual eyes will awaken and do their job. They will tell you where you are and where you are going. You will begin to be whole. That means you will begin to use every part of you as a whole unit. Why do you think Jesus said to the blind woman, "Your faith has made you whole"? Because she closed her eyes, knew where she was because her faith lit her within, and she knew where she was to go. Then she became whole or healed.

Do you see, this is a three-step process? Wholeness comes from using the spiritual with the physical. Generally, people only use 20% spiritual energy and 80% physical energy. When you balance this, healing, miracles, and more begins to happen to you. Then, when you go 80% spiritual and 20% physical, well let's just say, you ascend or transcend completely into the highest levels of heaven. Many have sought to obtain this shift, but very few find it. Why do you think the Bible says that the road to heaven is straight and narrow and few will find it, but the road to Hell is wide and many will find it? Hell represents the place that is lower than the highest heavens. Many souls can incarnate from some upper levels of Hell and lower levels of Heaven. So, to come down here as a soul and completely ascend is unusual because it takes lifetimes of learning to ascend properly. Jesus came down to Earth to teach you how to ascend faster and easier. He came to "save" you, but save you from what? Hell or the lower levels. To save you from not ascending to where you need and want to be. He came to teach the world and was the sacrifice sent to balance the energy and open an easier path to heaven.

It will do you no good to worship Jesus every day and say you love him, but not understand his teachings. It is learning the soul needs to ascend. Why do you think the Bible was even put together? As a sort of guide to help you learn faster. Why do you think this book is being written? Because millions of people, souls, have asked for a better understanding, and they need something more. God will most certainly answer you or give it to you if you ask.

Now, are you in understanding? It is not what you can do for the Lord at first but what the Lord can do for you. Then and only then can you serve and know what purpose you have and what you are serving. As the song goes "I loved you because you first loved me."

Your soul has to learn a higher way. The only way to learn is for it to be shown. So, then, why do you see people who get ugly and say nasty, hurtful things? Because they need to be shown. The next time someone is hateful, show them love. What are you scared of? Rejection or acceptance? If they reject your gift, your love will simply return back to you. If they accept it, then it will begin to bloom and grow. Praise the Lord; the outcome for you is good either way! Why? Because you have acted out of the purest love, which is Spirit. Amen.

> *"Angels are principally the guardians of our spirits.*
> *Their function is not to do our work for us,*
> *but to help us do it ourselves, by God's grace."*
> —EILEEN ELIAS FREEMAN

Angel Ambriel

It's Your Sandwich and You Can Build It How You Want

I want to talk to you about the "turkey sandwich." Yes, I said, "turkey sandwich." Picture a huge buffet. Let's say twenty large tables. All you can eat. See yourself as the first one in line. You take your plate, your napkin, and the twenty tables are fixed for every sandwich known to man. You just happen to prefer turkey. There are slices of the plumpest, juiciest turkey right off the bone. You come to the cheese, and you happen to like provolone. Now, the dressings, tomatoes, lettuce, onions, pickles, etc. And finally the bread. You choose a fresh French bread. You take your seat and begin to look at others around you. All of the ham sandwiches are sitting together, all of the Italian subs are cloistered in the corner table, and you, well, feel as if you are alone until all the other turkey sandwiches are finally sitting around you. Now, you feast, talk, laugh, cry, and rejoice until you notice the others around you and begin to judge your sandwich right or wrong.

Tell me, does this make any sense? NO! So then why do you judge other religions and belief systems?

It is because the turkey sandwich is not all God created. Instead of thinking God made a religion or school that would help teach your soul, you begin to think you are lacking, then comes fear, judgment, condemnation, and separation. . . . Do you see? The meat is the word, yes, the word. Some use the Bible, some use the Gnostic texts, others use the Catholic text. Yet God created all this meat. The cheese is the way you act or believe. Example: cheddar could be that you are more bitter or harsh in your faith; provolone could be that you are very quiet yet faithful like a monk or nun. The dressings or fixings are the adornments you choose. Crosses, prayer beads, singing, praising, etc. And the bread? Well, this holds everything together.

This is love. Real love. Not just shallow, physical love. We are talking real unconditional love, and many will go through the line and never pick it up. You see the buffet is spread. You can have as much as you want. It is you who picks and chooses. Those who supposedly worship Satan, or never know who they are, are starving themselves. They feel like they don't deserve it, and all they feel is destruction and lack. You decide.

Do you realize you deserve or do you choose lack? Whatever you choose, remember you spread it. Why spread lack?

I will leave you with this today: Do not choose according to what your soul thinks it deserves. Lay this to the side. Choose what you really are. Spirit, the image of God. Created and not lacking. "Why?" you ask. Because, shining one, this is who you really are! Amen!

"When hearts listen, angels sing."
—ANONYMOUS

Angel Meriah

Do Not Fear Family Karma

Greetings to all of you today who have chosen to read this book. You will be inspired, uplifted, and set on a new path.

Today we are going to talk about people. People reproducing people. But not just people, people's family karma. Now, I know many of you are thinking of your own family and what has transpired since you have been on the Earth. We are talking about what some people call "negative family energy" or "sins of the forefathers," or past family karma. Can this be energetically passed down one to another? Yes!! Is there really anything to christening a child to cleanse past sins or prayers to stop the cycle? Yes! You see, we are going to take a cabbage, for instance. If you grow a cabbage that has a tendency toward easily acquiring mold on its leaves, and then you take and reproduce it, what do you think you have just passed down? The same negative effect genetically. Also, there was a weakness in its energy field or what we will call its mind/emotional field.

Let's say the weakness is because you screamed and yelled at it every day. Do you think that the next generation has a chance to fully bloom, develop, and grow without negative results? No! It will be passed down unless something is done to consciously change this. Love it more. Change its water, soil, and nutrients, and PLEASE stop yelling. It will wilt right before your eyes. Go ahead and try it. There has to be a conscious effort to change the new ones being created. So, you see this is very much real in your dimension. Now in human terms, how are we going to change family energy or karma? Be aware consciously not to make the same previous steps. Go within and find your own path, not your uncle's or father's or your aunt's way. This life or walk is about you. You have to find you and your link before you can consciously do all the things you were sent down here to do.

Why do you think you set up schools or colleges? It was

to focus on the individual child and help them find their path. Unfortunately, there are all kinds of confusion and obstacles to prevent this, and not all of them will get it at first. Eventually they will. When you find your path, you will see that it begins to wind and intermix with all others and that they all come from Source. Sort of like an octopus with billions of tentacles. Sometimes you think you are the only tentacle in the ocean. Not knowing your Source, you are very lonely and afraid. Sometimes you are with other tentacles, but you do not know your Source. Sometimes you are alone or with others, but you do know the Source. How do you know? You follow your trail all the way up or within yourself until you find the body, or Source, or God. Now, you know the truth.

Now you know where you come from. Now you know where all of "it" originates from. Wouldn't it be silly to say, "I am the only tentacle, and there is no Source that I am attached to." Wow! That is living in a state of denial. So, for all of you who are atheist and assume you are "it," you just haven't followed the trail up. When you see that you have a Source, you understand that everything that you need is provided for. "It" will move you, no matter what you want, because "it" is in control.

For some of you this is scary because you feel if you are not 100% in control, something you deem as bad will happen, and you do not want to experience that. Don't you understand that in your life something you deem as bad is going to happen anyway so that you can grow? But if you are connected or know Source, really it will always be okay. Do you understand? You are connected whether you like or not, and that is the fact! If you don't see it now, you will when you are out of the body.

Family karma, why did it begin? Well, it was like energetically passing off the baton to the next runner. The thing is, you need to figure out if that baton is worth running for or with. Many of you don't know that you can change your baton. For example, George Smith is an alcoholic who is afraid of the world and doesn't know if he can find God and doesn't know if he wants to. He runs and runs with his baton. Two children are born to him, Joseph and Michael. Joseph is handed the baton and tries to run with it. He doesn't care for it but assumes the position anyway. Now he has become addicted and passes the baton to his son. Michael, on the other hand, doesn't like the baton. He realizes his choice to run with it is just that, and he leaves the race to go and look for a worthy baton to finish with. He grabs a baton full of grace, love, forgiveness, and truth.

Now he is running and then he passes the baton to his son. He just broke the cycle or the family karma. Do you see you chose your family for lessons, but your choice is to be like them or change the pattern? This is your choice. Today, evaluate your family. Are the values, thoughts, and beliefs worthy of running with? Are they the truth? If not, you might want to trade it in for one that is. Don't forget Source will supply you with as many different kinds of batons as desired. The choice is yours! May each of you today break forth a new song. A song of truth, love and purity. A song of healing and mindful intent. Blessed are those who thirst. Amen.

> *"A man does not always choose*
> *what his guardian angel intends."*
> —THOMAS AQUINAS

Angel Anthyus

Put First Your True Existence

Today being a new day, we will begin with a quote from the Bible from Matthew 6:19–20: "Do not lay up for yourselves treasures on Earth, where thieves break in and steal; but lay up for yourselves treasures in heaven, where neither moth nor rust destroys and where thieves do not break in and steal." Newness does not necessarily lie within the confines of a mind, but with the start of each new day.

You see, you may not be mindful of a new beginning, but it happens anyway. Your mind may be stuck on past issues, and really, unless they are for lessons or love, they are irrelevant. Don't hover over that which you cannot change. If you try to, you are just holding on to yesterday. Things of the past matter not. Again, only if you can learn from it or if it's supplied you with love or gave you love, is it important to remember. Real love, Spirit love, unconditional love, lets go. It does not hold on. Decide what you will do each day with all of the newness of the sun shining in your face. Each day is an adventure—a trial or test to see how you are existing. Are you getting that no one should hold on? We should allow in change and newness even if it completely changes our environment.

Do not attach to treasures or material possessions that you would want to cling to in order to validate who you are. You do not need any adornments. You are beautiful, just as the light you are. All of the other stuff takes away and hides your light. Many people try to be great successes in this life based on monetary possessions. Why do they not understand that these possessions are temporary, and so is their greatness based on this? Their greatness is the light and love within them. You see, all is well that ends well, and the fall of greatness in monetary possessions rarely ends well. Let's take two houses, for example. Both are grand, fine homes. One is great with a red-brick facing, arched windows, and airy ceilings. Strong, sturdy, powerful. The other house is made of largeness. A white exterior, grand halls, tile floors, and openness.

In the first house, the occupants base their greatness on their wealth. They buy and buy but never seem to be satisfied. Their house is cold and empty. The white house is large so that it can hold a large family. Knowing who they are, being loving, charitable, and forgiving, they fill the house with their warmth, and so it radiates out to everyone who comes by. Which house is full and which house is empty? Both are houses. Do you see that the things around you reflect the energy you give it? Greatness is wonderful—if you know where greatness comes from and that all beings of light are reflections of God's greatness. Then you value everyone and everything. You see prosperity is a blessing, but basing yourself on prosperity is wrong because you are not who you are based on these things.

Every time you build layers on top of your true existence, life will tear them down until you put your true existence first. Then you can build from that. Life will urge, encourage, shove, and move you toward who you really are. Why do you think there is death? Why do you think there are tragedies? To help you find your true self. Do not hold on to something so tight that it would destroy you to lose them, because everything will fade and disappear with time, but the true self! You are on a treasure hunt down here, and what you are hunting for is your true self. The goal of everyone should be what you humans call enlightenment or Nirvana or transformation. In other words, you have found you! And you are connected, a part of the one true Source—all that is and is to come. You cannot run, hide, or escape the truth. For it will find you . . . Amen.

"There is a land, where the roses are without thorns, where the flowers are not mixed with brambles. In that land, there is eternal spring, and light without any cloud. The tree of life groweth in the midst thereof; rivers of pleasures are there, and flowers that never fade. Myriads of happy spirits are there, and surround the throne of God with a perpetual hymn. The angels with their golden harps sing praises continually, and the cherubim fly on wings of fire! This country is Heaven . . . "

—ANNA LAETITIA BARBAULD

Jesus (Energy with White Dove over the Head)

You Are Not the Vessel, but the Essence That Is Contained Within

Hello. All is well that ends well. You see many only remember my crucifixion and become angry and bereft, but it is my resurrection that all should remember. For we will all be resurrected and walk the Earth for a short time after our deaths. For I was born of the true light, and I never forgot this; therefore, I returned to my original state: true transformation.

41

However, there are many who do not transform, who send themselves according to their will to a painful Hell. Hell is being in a state of not transforming into the beauty of the light. In other words, you seem separate when you are supposed to be part of the "whole" or the "flock." Many who have written the Bible were inspired by God, but it is very difficult for the body and mind to find the words to describe the Spirit.

The body is born from Spirit or God, but it only contains part. For example, think of a blue vase. The vase is the body; the cork in the top is the mind. The emotional body is the color of the vase. Now, the Spirit is the liquid within the vase. What is the most valuable part? And can the glass truly know all of the liquid and where it came from? It only knows how it feels to hold the liquid, and it sees where it is poured. Do you understand? Your body is no more capable than the glass vase of knowing and understanding value.

So, then, how do you think that there are exact words to describe Spirit since the words are coming from the body, and the body can't possibly know all? Why do you take so much literally into the words? There will always be more that will be said or taught or written to explain the Bible's Word. Why then do you scoff at other writings? Because it is written that you should not add to or take away from the Bible? The "add to" was put in by man as a symbol of control. God did not only speak to us in my times. God speaks to all every day in the existence of this world, and God will continue to speak. Do not ask the container to do what it cannot do. You humans expect the body to do more, know more, be more. All the body should do or do first is know that what is within it is the true light. The Source. True light from true light! Once it knows this, then it values the trueness first, and then it values itself, because it has an important job: to carry around the True Light. When your value is on truth, your vessel reflects, emanates, and radiates what is within: love, light, and acknowledgment of other vessels of light.

If you are to teach your children anything, it is who they are! Remind them that they are not the vessel, but the essence that is contained within. Preachers, teachers, it is your responsibility to know this and teach this.

When I was crucified, many wept and are still weeping. It was as if a giant, large bottle was crushed many times over for all the world to see. But it was my essence that was freed. My body's death had to be so violent and documented so that the point would be made that no human can destroy the true light. It was to take away your fear, not to create it, but if you see yourself as the vessel and not the true light, it will scare you.

Do you not see my last attempt was to give you the last great understanding of who you are? That is what will save you. The true light. I was chosen as part of the true light to walk the Earth. I came into a vessel that always knew what the truth was. I did not have to be taught. That is why we differ. When I said, "All that will go to the Father must go through me and all that accepts the Father accepts me." That means that in order to see truth, God, you must see who I am. I am true light, but guess what? SO ARE YOU! By seeing me, you should begin to see yourself, because I was a teacher who was here to teach you the greatest truth. Yourself! When John said that he was not fit to carry my sandals, it was because he, or his emotional being, judged his vessel as not as worthy as mine, because he had to be taught.

The death of John's vessel was not easy either. But was he not as worthy? You see, if you would value your true self, there would be no inferiority, no insecurity, no fear, no dread. Do not bother with the things that feed your falseness, lies, and opinions. But bother with the things that reflect the light and truth so that it will help you to see your own. We will speak again soon. There are many lessons the vessel needs to know. Amen.

> *"Believers look up—take courage.*
> *The angels are nearer than you think."*
> —BILLY GRAHAM

Angel Semon

Message to the Author

Welcome back! You were chosen as an imperfect state, so that true perfection can come through you and be seen. Do not feel lazy or as if you do not do enough. For when you sleep, you do not completely rest, but hold massive amounts of energy for the journey. Why do you think your children and spouse want to sleep by you and near you? Because of the energy you store. You are a container full of the blessed holy energy, as all humans could be if they allow it.

You want to know how you differ from Mother Teresa? She had more faith, she did not doubt herself after she got clear guidance from the Holy Council, and she had more compassion. You have more room for improvement, but don't all human forms? I want to talk to you today about your work, and it is imperative. You write this down and listen! You are merely a conduit for the Source to run through. Isn't that what you're told? What does the "you" mean in this instance? It is the human form. Now, the human form is not the real you! You should know that by now. The real you is your Spirit, but the mind, body, and ego have to humble themselves for the real you to come forth. When the real you, or Spirit, steps forward, miracles will happen. As with prophets and disciples, it is no great shift as one would expect, but ever so slightly that one day sightings of these miracles will begin, and woe to those who persecute because they will be put through a similar fire or test. Do not hold on to karma. Let it merely hold on to you as a hair or string. When you see it, cut it loose or pull it off, and you will do this with love. It is that easy. Karma is really easy to fix. You just have to be aware that it has presented itself to you.

Now, lessons are different. They cannot be cut or plucked off but learned—learned by the soul and the body. You will continue to get the testing of the lessons until you pass. Then, it is over. Your life will be filled with lessons, karmic restitution, and unexplained phenomenon. For this is your path. You are never to get too comfortable in this world, for your mission lies on the other side. You came to fulfill a quest. Your quest is to get out as much Spirit truth and then to return home. That's it! Sounds easy? Why do you think you can see and hear us Angels? Because we are one of your tools to fix non-reality and lies. We are a tool of truth.

You are to leave a major impact on this world, but you cannot do it alone. You will only arrive when you have humbled yourself—which, by the way, you are working on diligently, and God sees this. Your Spirit is functioning at about 45% now or one-fourth of its energy. Can you imagine 75% or 90%? There would be no room for shortcuts or small gains—only here for the cause. Yes, you will attain this one day, and then you will return home. You have a heavenly house waiting for you filled with light, peace, and more than the mind can comprehend, for it would blow all of its circuits.

How often should you go to God in prayer? As often as you have thoughts. Yes, your thoughts, mind, and emotions are like radar. However, this radar should be tuned as a prayer so that you are mindful at all times of your existence. Meditation creates mindfulness. Mindfulness creates right or high vibrational creation. To God be the glory. Amen.

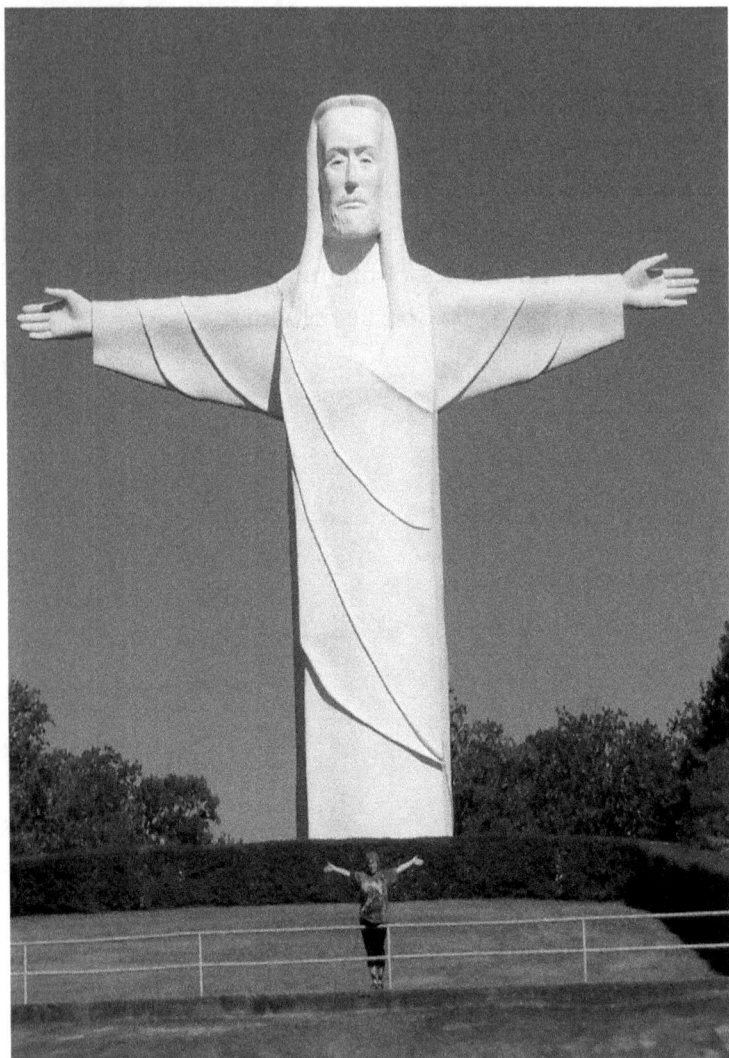

"But if these beings guard you, they do so because
they have been summoned by your prayers."

—AMBROSE

Jesus

Everyone Has a Destiny

Let us talk about sin! What is sinfulness? It is the ability to separate the body from the higher mind and the body from spirituality. Notice I said *the ability*? I did not say *the act.* Why? Because, as you say, you are born with sin or into sin. Therefore, each and every one of you has sin and/or the ability to sin. It is your will that allows it to manifest or not. So, your will is responsible for the action you take. Where does the will reside? It resides in your heart. Yes, your heart. This is why it is so important to have a purified heart. What does this mean? It means that your heart has merged with your spiritual heart and thus becomes purified. To God, be the glory. What do you think the pictures of me with the "sacred heart" represent? I was the only human to walk the Earth who was not born into sin. My heart (where the will resides) was always merged with God and, therefore, sacred or consecrated or absolute. I could not have conquered or overcome the world without that true oneness with God.

I was a teacher. I was sent to help you understand why you came and what you should do while you are here. I came to teach you responsibility for your actions. I also taught, among many other things, how to co-create with God—this leading to what you call miracles. Miracles begin when you get in sync with God. There are two things everyone must know down here on the Earth. *Number one:* Your path is your

49

path. It belongs to no one else but you. This is why your bodies are not all joined together. This is why God created separate bodies or "holding tanks" for your Spirit. Because if all of you were joining, you would not accomplish your destiny. What is destiny? Your goal, your obtainable goal that is set before you.

Many of you see destiny as a pole-vault competition. You will vault till you get no higher and quit. I say, and God says, when you co-create with the One, you can vault as high as you were meant to. You're like a helium balloon. You are the balloon, and God is the helium. God is what brings you up and rise to become what your destiny was to be. Why do you choose a destiny? So that your work is accomplished for your soul path. Or, in other words, you are born walking your path. You have to walk to the end to go home.

Destiny is the actual act of walking toward your goal or coming home. Everyone has destiny. Whatever begins has to end, and whatever ends has to begin. This is a universal law of Spirit on this plane of thought. *Number two:* Now, let's talk about spirituality. What does this mean? It means to be aware that you have or possess a Spirit. Spirit is the only thing you are until you come into this plane, which you so carefully helped to create. When you come into the body, it is a constant battle of who has control—Spirit (God, light, high-self, etc.) or body (ego, mind, emotion, the doorway for destruction to enter). The body represents a wild stallion, and the Spirit is the rider.

Can you tame the stallion, and if so, how will you do it? Think about the picture of the American Indian warrior mounted on a horse. His hands are reaching to the sky, to God. The horse's head is down in submission. It is standing still. That represents a Spirit taming the body. Your body has to be taught. Real wisdom is discerning whether a certain thought or emotion is Spirit or body. When you can discern the difference, you have conquered the first great horse. For now, I want you to understand that the first concept is to know thyself. You find out who you are by being shown religion and church. This should help you to see that your Source is God.

You should begin to see that you are not a human, not the horse, but the Spirit or the rider. How will you tame your horse? What will you use? Will you beat it, whip it, and scream and yell at it as many religions have taught you to do? Or will you love it, care for it, and let it earn your trust? Will you become a horse whisperer, or spiritual communicator, for the body? Every horse is different, and every body is different.

Today's lesson is about realization. Who are you? Who are you really? Do you know that you are the light? The light is you, and one day you will all know this. Many who do not know who they are scoff at this reality and light. They think they are the body and should be punished! I tell you surely as you see the truth, you shall see yourself and the real face of God. Here in form, in all forms. Creating and co-creating. Pray and ask God to anoint you with eyes that can see. Pray and ask God to help you know who you are and why you came here. Then pray and ask God to help you tame the body so that you can merge the body and soul with that of God's. Pray for the Immaculate Conception, that being the purpose God put into the body, for it to carry and birth. Then pray to come home. These are your steps to truth or enlightenment, or some say Nirvana. Amen.

Angel Ambriel

Align Yourself with the Will of God

I have come to set you free! Free from what you ask? Free
from your cares. I am here to show you exactly where you
should place your cares: at the Spirit's doorstep. For there are
so many things the physical body cannot accomplish, so it is
the Spirit's responsibility to accomplish. Then, when you lay
down these cares and woes, then and only then, will they get
fixed. The longer you hold on to them, the more they seem to
stick to you like glue—superglue, by the way, that may never
seem to want to separate. Did you know that as long as you
are in "the will" of God, all things will be accomplished? So,
then, if you are in "the will," why would you worry? You
would worry about the end for nothing. How many of you, on
a daily basis, base your worries on how you are physically
feeling? Bad choice, don't you think? What does it mean to

be in "the will"? It means hooking into God, walking your anointed path, and letting go of things you cannot control. Did I make that clear? Letting go!

Do you want to know how to get into "the will"? Ask that God will show you and then allow whatever it takes to put you there. This may be easy on you or very hard. But when you are in "the will," you will know it because you will have peace like you have never known. Great sages, healers, and prophets know that to be in "the will," is the greatest secret, or gift, one could give to the body, mind, and heart. That means letting go of what you are or, in this case, the body. Surrender! *Carpe Diem*—seize the day—or, in other words, reach out and grab the light, but you will have to let go of the world to do this. Not everyone understands.

Job went through a testing or being in "the will." He was in God's will, and the test came. Was Job to hold on to what God had given and hold on so much that he could not let go when God had removed it? Or was he, as painful as it was, to let go of what was given and accept that which came next? What did he do? He went through a painful process or pit in the path of letting go and staying in "the will." And he did. Of course, you know all that he loved was restored more than it was before. Why did God allow this pit in the road? Because Job chose to be the example of letting go in choosing the high path. The high road is not always easy on the body. This is why being long suffering is a virtue or a gift your Spirit gives to the body to help it endure "the will" of God. Really, God's will is the will of your Spirit because your Spirit is part of God.

So you are choosing as you have from the beginning of the beginning. Lay down your burdens. Only then will you see the face of God in yourself, in your mirrors. These mirrors exist within everyone so that they see the truth. Ego and prideful love transform into light because you bring them deep within to your true self. The more ego you dissipate, the more you can reflect the light from within. Peace be to all who read this. Amen!

Angel Aureneal

God Is Mother and Father

Hope. What is hope and why do we have it? Hope was devised when the first Spirit jumped into the soul and then both jumped into the body. The core emotion is hoping that one can achieve the goal and return home. Hope that all has been said and will be done at the appropriate time. Hope is for those who know that there will be a tomorrow and that tomorrow will be as it should. Hope is knowing that everything returns to its Source, God. If you have no hope, then you fool yourself into thinking that there is no God and that is simply incorrect! If there was no God, what would be the point of your existence? Some of you say there is no God, so therefore you are saying there is no you. You also know this is untrue!

God should be as obvious to you as you are if you look in a mirror. If you say there is no God, this is called denial. Denial was created to teach all of those who choose not to believe. You can only deny so long before you have to see what really is. Truth. God. Very simple, yes? Do you believe in the Trinity? FATHER, SON, HOLY SPIRIT or TRUTH, INTEGRITY, COMPASSION or LIGHT, LIGHT EMANATING ON EARTH, THE WAY OF THE LIGHT or FAITH, HOPE, LOVE or FATHER, CHILD, MOTHER. Ah ha! I am sure you never thought of this one! Don't you know that there is a Source that nurtures, loves, gives, nourishes, and mends? You humans see this role as female. Then why, if there are females on Earth, do you say everything comes from God in HIS image? Why wouldn't God also be part feminine? You cannot say God is this but not that. If everything comes from God and returns from God, then why isn't God everything? Why have you killed one another over what God truly is?

The way to find the truth about God is to get on your knees, pray, meditate, and forget what so much of the world pushes you to believe. Jesus referred to God as Father. Yes, God is part Father but also part Mother. In his role, Jesus needed the male or masculine energy to help him achieve all that he was to do. Most of his mothering came from Mary, who by the way, was to some extent pure form of God incarnate upon the Earth. You, as a single human with a soul and Spirit, are attracted to the facet of God that will help you achieve your goal down here. Why do you think people have died for the God they see? Because to them it is their truth, and only by truth will you achieve your purpose. Everyone should support the part of God they see as long as it is truth, and others should celebrate them for doing this.

Each one of you should have your own personal relationship and path. The teachers in your life are there, either to cause pain and sorrow or to bring light and joy to you. Either way, you will learn "trueness." You are to follow no man but to walk with him or beside him if you share his belief. There will be times when there is chaos, and there will be times when there is joy. Both are there to teach you the truth. Do not be afraid; only be aware. Being aware is about knowing what your truth with God in this life is and what is not. For example, Catholics and Protestants: one has the holy consecration (communion) and one does not, according to the Catholics. Have you ever thought that the ones who are following the Catholic road desperately need the holy consecration and the ones on the Protestant road do not? If they did, they would be Catholic.

How dare you humans condemn another faith because of your shortsightedness! You do not know all of the ways of God. Don't you realize that God is a builder? God will build many, many roads to get you back home, but they all lead to God (Father/Mother). If you had any idea the love God contains, you would be shocked that you have not yet acknowledged, asked for it, and passed it on to others. One day you will all learn the value of Spirit. When you do, there will truly be a new Heaven and new Earth. Amen!

> *"Around our pillows golden ladders rise,*
> *And up and down the skies,*
> *With winged sandals shod,*
> *The angels come and go,*
> *The messengers of God!"*
>
> —RICHARD HENRY STODDARD

Jesus

Everything Comes from the One True Source

How are you today? Do you have despair? Do you seem lost, lonely, or sad? Many of you are looking for the light. It awaits you within yourself. It is like an angel with a candle, leading you within yourself to the truth. Truth and knowledge. Truth and understanding await you there. There is no darkness, ignorance, or destruction that can argue with the truth. It merely dissipates in the light. Now, no two birds are exactly alike, just like no two souls are exactly the same. Because of experiences, karma, and soul contracts, you are all different. But the truth that lies within, or your Spirit, is the same. It never changes, and it is always there. This is God from where you came. Truth and knowledge.

If the soul wants to know, it should ask the Spirit. It seems as if so many of you get caught up in the words, so much so that you lose the meaning of why you truly exist. If I were to tell you, you would not believe me, or maybe many of you have been waiting for the opportunity to know who you are. Many of you think that you are just a body with a head or mind attached. I tell you that is simply the "machine" or "holding tank." In order to fulfill your purpose, you need to know who you are. Why is it important to know who you are? Because you will be pulled in many different directions when you do not know the truth. But when you see truth, you are no longer pulled. You are all placed down here together to show one another the TRUTH. You reflect and refract off one another. By doing this, you seem to find the one true Source. Everything comes from the one true Source. Nothing more, nothing less. When you are sad, turn to Source. Happy, turn to Source. Depressed, turn to Source. Angry, turn to Source. Neglected, turn to Source. If you make this your immediate reaction, you will lack for nothing.

Everyone has the ability to heal, but not everyone chooses too. LOVE IS ALL THERE IS. It heals, changes, aligns, resets; it just is. You see, I showed the disciples over and over and over how to love. Miracles, they are just tiny shreds of love. Forgiveness, shreds of love. Prayer and meditation, shreds of love. If you want to do something nice, love yourself. Why, in this society of humans, do you think that neglecting the body is an act of love? Self-punishment—what for? I tell you, love, real love is pure, and when you show real love to your body, your body will respond with amazing results.

Now, do you know yet who you are? You are Source. For example: Imagine God as the sun with Jesus and the Christ consciousness at the center. You are a ray of light jumping off the Source point, coming to Earth to shine, and then to bounce back to Source, and then to bounce back again. You see, your purpose is to shine. "Shine how?" you ask. Just as every snowflake is different, so is every bounce of your light ray. So shine for your purpose in each life. You will know this by getting quiet and bringing prayer and meditation into your surroundings.

Are there people, places, or things that need the light? Give the light to them. You have as much as you will ever need. No matter where you are, shine so that you can help others remember they are rays of light also. Do you need to know why you shine? Because that is all there is to do. Very simple. Very easy. Just be.

> Twinkle twinkle, little ray.
> How I wonder what you are.
> Filled within the light today,
> point me God, I ask and pray.
> Set me on the path of light,
> so that I might reflect what you are for sight.
> Know that now I have found my way.
> A light I will be for today.

Nothing more, nothing less—just light. Amen.

> *"When my time to die comes an angel will be there to comfort me. He will give me peace and joy even at that most critical hour, and usher me into the presence of God, and I will dwell with the Lord forever. Thank God for the ministry of His blessed angels."*
>
> —BILLY GRAHAM

Saint Francis

Understand the Rhythms of the Body

Hello. I have so much to say, and yet will try to formulate the words and meanings so that understanding can come easily for you. Many of you are having heart and vascular issues. What is the meaning of this? There has been an increase in heart failure, arrhythmias, and palpitations. Many of you who have these issues are having a difficult time with what is and what has been. You are longing for an experience that has already been. You reach backward instead of forward so that the rhythms of the body become imbalanced. The heart, mind, and soul have their own rhythms. The heart rhythm beats each beat within the moment. It does not beat in the past nor in the future. All it knows to beat for is now. So, whenever the emotional body requires attention based on past or future events and this is not acknowledged, it will simply pull on a "rope" and trigger the heart to beat out of rhythm so that attention can be given. Picture a woman pulling on a rope to summon a servant. Don't you see that the two are directly linked? Stop, drop to your knees or sit and acknowledge what the emotional body wants. When things go too far, the heart has an attack, and if the soul wills, it will leave the body to die, keeping in mind that the issue was not resolved. If it cannot be settled in other dimensions, then it will have to incarnate again. Now, the mind beats to another rhythm. More on a soul level, which we will talk about in a moment. The mental aspect of the mind is to work out every obstacle diligently, thoroughly, and with progress.

When people become mentally lazy or they seem to be stuck in a process and feeling as if no progress has been made, then the mind rhythms change. The mind can go from past to present to future, but when these feelings occur or physical changes occur, the rhythms either shift to past or future. This is mostly because the past is familiar and has processed the event as being allowed. Take, for example, Alzheimer's disease. Yes, there are many, many causes to Alzheimer's disease, but what is the root cause? It is an offbeat mental rhythm. How do you correct this? Ask the mind what has thrown off its rhythm . . . yes, simple, easy yet effective. The mind will tell you if you ask.

Why do you think hypnotherapy works if a person is open? If you were completely open, you could ask the mental body yourself, and you could hear its answer. The same applies to the heart. What does *open* mean? It means first, not having any fear; second, you have no preconceived ideas; and third, you trust with all of your heart. Did you know that fear is stored in the brain? The brain hands out tidbits of fear here and there when it sees fit. Trust and faith are stored within the heart. The more trust and faith you have, the more open and healthy your heart is. The less fear you have, the more balanced and fearless your mind is. Do not confuse real fear with conditioned fear. Real fear is your brain telling you to move off the tracks or the train will hit you. This fear is given by the Spirit to keep the body surviving so that Spirit and soul can fulfill its purpose.

This is good fear. It can come from the mental body, which remembers past lifetimes and tragedies, or it can come from this lifetime. It can be an event or a superimposed fear from parental or outside programming. For example, when you were two years old, your mother was shot and killed, but you were saved. Now, when you hear a gunshot or fireworks, your feelings are triggered and you may feel vulnerable, guilty because you lived, or just full of fear on whatever level. Here is another example: Your mother told you not to go down by the creek because you might get bitten by a snake. Now, when you are around water, you are full of anxiety or very nervous. The point to all of this is to find your root.

Ask your mental body the following: 1) Is this fear from a past lifetime? 2) Is this fear conditioned? 3) Is this fear from this lifetime tragedy? When you find the root, then you can take a therapeutic point of view to heal the wound. In our suffering comes our greatest exploration. If you had no suffering, you would think that this body and this Earth are all that exists. Through suffering, you find truth. Now, this is the soul rhythm. A soul has a rhythm of its own but can merge or become any other rhythm. It is not considered good or bad;

it just is. So, whenever someone has cancer, and it has been derived or created from a change in the soul rhythm, the soul chose this for a reason. This is considered sacred suffering. You suffer to find truth and to help others find truth. Think about the stigmata. Stigmata means suffering for a higher spiritual purpose. So, some who are spiritually open, as I was in that body, may actually bear the wounds of Christ. Or if you do not have that perception, then you may develop cancer or other issues. Now, here is the summation: disease = imbalance = rhythms have changed.

Look to:
First, Heart-emotional body
Second, Brain-mental body
Third, Soul—Soul/Spirit

This is where the root to all diseases exists. Search the Trinity to find your answer, then solution, then peace. God Bless All of You, Amen!

Angel Angelica

Lose Opinions and Reshape Your Clay

Good day. I am Angel Angelica, giver of treasures of the heart. I am here today to speak with all of you about right and wrong. Is there such a thing and does it only exist in this plane? Well, the answer is yes, yes, no. In other words, yes it exists, yes in this plane, but no, not only in this plane. You see, humans needed a word or meaning for, "I manifested or created something I do not want or did not mean too." Humans also needed a word to describe, "Yes, yes, yes, that is exactly what I meant to create." Hence, the words *wrong* and *right*. Now, unfortunately, humans believe that God only creates that which is exactly what God meant to do, simply because God doesn't make mistakes. So God is right or good. The Spirit is directly linked or connected to God and made in the image of the I AM.

Humans create a lot of things that they were not ready for.

65

So, we deem these mistakes. For example: teenage pregnancy, overdose, substance abuse, etc. I did not say these things were mistakes, but that is how so many humans see them. Have you ever thought that there are no mistakes? Really? Think about a ball of clay. If you form it into a shape that is not appealing to you, don't you reform it and learn from this? You can ALWAYS reshape the clay just like your life or what you are creating down here. Why do so many of you condemn yourself when you do this? Is it because those around you have opinions of your form, and then, so do you? Precisely. Think back to Adam and Eve. When they saw they were not clothed, they felt ashamed and covered themselves with fig leaves. Who felt ashamed first? Adam. Why? Because he was created the first male form. Why do you think there are more male preachers and so many believe "the father should be the head of the family." It was because Adam had the first opinion and taught Eve his version of wrong. Do you understand? Do you want a programmed hundred years of wrong, or do you want the truth?

Truth is, there are no mistakes and no right or wrong. There only *is,* like the ball of clay. If you do not like it, reshape it. So many of you get stuck in the thought, "I messed up. I am a horrible person." Then when you believe this label, you continue the process. It is your choice. However, you could see it as, "I created this by this choice, and I don't like this, so I will reshape and change." Then and only then will all of you become perfection—when you lose opinions and reshape. Take, for example, the adulteress brought to Jesus by the disciples. Did Jesus say kill her? Did Jesus say flog her, judge her, condemn her? NO! Jesus said first to the disciples, "Who among you is without sin? Let him cast the first stone." Or in other words, "The one of you who hasn't molded your clay into a form you didn't care for can kill her." Simply, there was no one. Then Jesus said, "Go and sin no more," or in other words, "Reshape your clay, erase this form."

Now she can be set free to obtain perfection. Simple, right? It is all about change. When should we change and how? That is always within you. Your Spirit knows what shapes to make for your path. Ask your Spirit. It is directly connected or linked or is the image of God. This is the highest truth. People should not make art only because it is what other people want to see. People should make art because it is a true reflection of the True Spirit within them. In other words, don't be shaped by others opinions. Be shaped by the inner desire for the truth. Then you will create a masterpiece. God keep you all of your blessed days upon the Earth. Amen!

> *"Praise the Lord, you his angels, you mighty ones
> who do his bidding, who obey his word."*
>
> —PSALM 103:20

Angel Isadora

---

*Don't Shield Yourself
from Love*

Love—isn't it appropriate that we should discuss this today. Of course, we will also discuss how love is used for light or dark and how we will always know the difference. Real love, true love, is like a fountain that never runs dry. Thousands, millions, billions will come and drink, and it will never run dry. How often do you envision this? You should see this every day in your morning prayers. Are you the fountain or are you the one who thirsts, and from where does the water come from? All in good time.

Now let's talk about the makeup or the composition of love. Not just in your dimension but also in ours. In your dimension, love wells up from somewhere within. That is from your Spirit. Your Spirit gives it and feels it freely. Yet, it has to go through the soul in order for the physical body to receive it. When it bypasses the soul and goes to the body, this is called a miracle. It seems to jump the current or leaps from another facet. This is a very interesting feature when this happens. Not everyone or everybody will experience this. This is a most powerful and extraordinary thing. Now, the soul almost seems to be like the skin. It absorbs in order for the body to receive it. Not everybody has "penetrable skin," you see. Many of you have become leather skinned like an alligator or an armadillo. You have armored yourself from the whole world, but in doing this, you armor yourself from the entire world of love.

Why would your soul and physical body want you to do this? Many of you do not realize you are doing this until it is too late. One should never have to shield oneself from love. This is how you know it is love. Because there is no need for protection. How many of you feel you need protection and if so from whom? Yourself? Really none can hurt you or harm you unless you give them permission to on some level. So then, if you are in control at all times (and you are, you just don't realize it), why would you need protection? I tell you to strip away the victim within you and step into your power of who you really are. When you do this, the ego and/or fear will melt away and only love will be left.

Love is an amazing thing really. It is eternal; you cannot harm it, kill it, hurt it, or destroy it. It is an absolute just like your Spirit. It has always been and will always be. Now, let's talk about the other vibrations that we want to call love. There is lust, greed, domination, vulnerability, self-destruction, loathing, and mayhem. Yes, believe it or not, you have one time or another labeled all of these as love. Why do you do this? Do you not understand? Love is like the sky; it is permanent. Rain clouds may come in and pollution may hang in the air, but the sky (or love) remains. Really, it is very untouched and secluded, beckoning you to come and float in it. No matter what, it will always remain. Whenever you have an emotion that you assume is love, I want you to ask yourself these four questions:

1. Does it hurt or cause harm on any level?

2. Does it give me peace?

3. Does it give my mind knowledge of who I really am?

4. Does it go on and on, never ceasing?

First of all love, never causes us harm or hurt. It pardons on all levels. It is not selfish or unkind. It never ceases, and in this "never ceasing" stands as a pillar of peace and a mountain of knowledge. Love is pure and true. It remains when all else has faded away. Love does not fear, nor does it have any acknowledgment of fear. In its truest form, it is absolute, and it remains as one of the pathways back home for you. Now, this brings us to the next level. Your passage back home. When you arrive at ground zero or the stripping down of who you think you are, and the understanding of whom you really may be, there are four noble paths home. You will always have a main theme with the other three mixed in. This main theme will be your totem pole or your flag that waves you on for your voyage home.

They are Love, Peace, Truth, and Faith.

The first noble path is Love. If one has love as their path, then they will be tested and retested if they can continue to love. No matter the abuse, no matter the fear, they will have to climb these mountains and take the path of love to get home. These mountains may be sexual abuse, drugs, or a disabled parent or child. In all of these situations, they will be challenged to love themselves and others. You have chosen the titles to your own mountains, and yes, you have put them there! You set these up ahead before you incarnate, as if you were challenging yourself and you set up an obstacle course.

The second noble path is Peace. Those who are on the path of peace usually have a peaceful life with the exception of some massive traumas. Sometimes the mountains seem so large they think they will never cross over. Some of these mountains may be the Native American Indian wars: Trail of Tears, slaughter of thousands, and reservation life. This person has chosen the path of peace that is very difficult and hard to walk, but they will find peace within themselves no matter what and ride over the mountains. The only fear is that the peace within them will be lost. These are our peacemakers. Blessed are the peacemakers for they shall inherit the Kingdom of God.

The third noble path is Truth. You, of course, will be given the task of seeking truth and staying on that path. When you climb the mountains, you will have a tendency to leave the path of truth to ascend or climb to half-truths or falseness. These mountains could be the thought that you are better than others, that your religion is the only one that will make it into heaven, or that you are not all equal in God's eyes. Of course, these mountains will vary from person to person, but now you can see that you have to climb these mountains of untruth to walk the truth. Very interesting. Usually, these people tend to have more epiphanies or revelations after they descend from the mountains.

The fourth noble truth is Faith. Now, these are the ones who are going to be tried and tested for what they believe. As long as they have faith in the real absolute, the one God, and all of God's absolute truths, they shall finish at heaven's gates. They are the ones who will study and really have to know the truth. When they do, they shall walk on water. This is quite a beautiful path. Some of these mountains could be fear of who they are, fear of being judged, or the fear of failing God. At the end, they shall see that just by incarnating and walking the path, they did not fail God.

This path can be extremely difficult, and one must know first who they are. The absolute truths are necessary for this path. Now, just for your information, Jesus walked all four paths in one lifetime! Jesus was the only one, who from the beginning to the end, walked, climbed, and endured all of the mountains. Of course, on each one of these paths, you will need the other three noble truths, but your theme will only be one. Which one are you? I come in Peace and Peace I leave with you. No one can alter, change, affect, or negate your path or your life. You are the giver of permission. Remember who you are!!

With Eternal Love, Isadora

"*I will not wish thee riches, nor the glow of greatness, but that wherever thou go some weary heart shall gladden at thy smile, or shadowed life know sunshine for a while. And so thy path shall be a track of light, like angels' footsteps passing through the night.*"

—WORDS ON A CHURCH WALL IN UPWALTHAM, ENGLAND

> "God will deign to visit oft the dwellings of just men,
> Delighted, and with frequent intercourse
> Thither will send his winged messengers
> On errands of supernal grace."
> —JOHN MILTON

Angel Josia

———————

Take the Pill of Laughter

Greetings! I am the bringer of laughter, or as you say, a clown. My form changes according to the will of the person, and I am here to explain what laughter is and why God made it. You see, in this land of balancing of light and dark, God knew there would be sorrow, fear, dread, and worry. God decided that he/she would give you an antidote for these. This little pill is called laughter. You all have an endless supply in your medicine cabinet. Yet, you act like to take one, you are an addict. Laughter is a formation or collage of three emotions. One being an absolute. Love (the absolute), light, and harmony. When you laugh, you inject yourself with a syringe of these three emotions, and this equals laughter. Now, do not be discouraged, but not all laughter comes from these emotions. You see, just as God created this, human ego created laughter too. However, its three emotions differ from the ones that God created in pure form. They are malice, jealousy, and revenge.

These three emotions equal a syringe of laughter but are, of course, not very progressive at all. The two can be compared as *Syringe A*—love, light, and harmony = all of the healing you could ever need or vitamins, enzymes, minerals etc. and *Syringe B*—malice, jealousy, and revenge = breakdown and destruction or injection of poison. Which one would you inject yourself with? You see, it comes down to your choice. Teach your children not to laugh at disabled people, but to laugh with joy with a disabled person about something of pure compassion and enjoyment.

Now, on to another topic . . . fear and dread. I will be short and to the point. Do you trust God? Do you trust your Spirit? Do you know you are eternal? Never ending? Do you realize who you are? If you answered yes to all of these, then you have no fear or dread.

God Bless and Keep you. Amen.

Apostle Paul

Are You a Buzzard or Are You a Dove?

Author's observation: He appears in the coat of many colors with the wings of an angel. This is not his normal appearance. I believe he has changed to prove a point or to give a lesson. This may be also indicative of his human/ Spirit nature. When we change out of our norm, it is to teach a lesson or prove a point.

Child, I come here today to teach you the story of all that is. You first looked at me, and your mind was unsure it was I, because you have known me first with your spiritual sight. When you discerned that it was I, you then began to process a reason for my appearance. Here is my first teaching today. Do not familiarize yourself with another's appearance or voice, even in the Spirit world with your Spirit eyes and ears.

You must first familiarize yourself with the sense of who they are. Your sense of knowledge of a presence will always be accurate. One can always appear or speak differently, but one can never change their true essence.

The coat falls off, and Jesus remains with angelic wings.

The next lesson, child, is that you can all fly, soar, and move. Not everyone has to show they have wings to fly. We all soar in different ways. Some soar close to the ground. Some leave straightaway. Some come and go as they will. You all need to become aware of how you soar and when. There is no right or wrong way. There just is, and you need to know this.

Many of you refuse to believe you can fly, while so many others of you want to do nothing but soar. If the heavenly father/mother made you a bird, then embrace that wingspan and use it to the best of who you embody. Are you a buzzard or are you a dove? Are you a hawk or a bluebird? Are you a raven or eagle? You see, the first question is not if you can fly, but what is the body you are placed in? Then when you know, you will know where and how to fly. My point is this: know thyself first! When you are aware of your own essence, then you will know to what depths and heights to fly.

When you are aware of yourself, then become aware of others—not their appearance or their voice, but their essence. Then you will always be aware on the deepest level and can never be fooled.

Jesus then takes off the whole appearance,
and it is St. Paul, the apostle.

You see I was clothed in other garments. You, author, were not so sure I was Jesus, but you chose to follow this through. It is because, author, you know the essence of Jesus. This is a lesson you would do well to learn. It will save you a lot of confusion. God bless and keep you. All in God's time . . . Amen.

> *"Christians should never fail to sense the operation of an angelic glory. It forever eclipses the world of demonic powers, as the sun does a candle's light."*
>
> —BILLY GRAHAM

Archangel Michael

Out of Everything Forceful Comes Something Gentle

Author's observation: Gentleness surrounds him as peaceful and soft as the feathers of a dove. He stands before me with a mighty sword in his hand. I know he is here to help all of mankind understand the light that is within. Never have I felt so much peace.

Hello. Why do you think I am the protector of the church? Because I am sent to bring peace. Many do not know this and assume I was created and born with this sword. I use the sword only to bring peace. You see, out of everything forceful comes something gentle. Out of every sword of action comes peace. Eventually. Your intent determines whether or not the peace comes now or later. All of you are born with a sword. Why? To see how and what you will use it for. Your sword will always tell and show you the way, but your intent drives it to move. It has no choice. It is at your will.

Do you think the cause or intent to move your sword is worthy? Will it suddenly bring peace? Where does peace come from? Truth. Truth of your existence. Truth of all existence. I ask, do you find yourself worthy of this sword? If not, then ask to be made worthy. Knowing how and when to use it. Don't you think the one writing this book is using her sword? She could channel anything she wanted, but she chose to use her sword for truth. Truth is God. Angels are messengers used to spread the truth. Her sword has been used for a worthy cause, and this will bring peace. Now do you understand? It is within that will show you how to swing the sword. What is within you is the light. What is the light? God and your Spirit coming together in a communion to move the sword. One that should be understood and learned.

You all need to go to "knight school." You pick up your sword and swing. Do you understand? This sword is truth. When you speak, live, and abide in the truth, you move this sword to bring peace. First, you have to know what truth is and where it originates. So if you have not entered "knight school," please sign up. Meditate, pray, learn, and listen within. Source will teach you. Swing your truth when you are ready. Pierce the darkness and find the light . . . Amen.

> "We can all be angels to one another. We can choose
> to obey the still small stirring within, the little
> whisper that says, Go. Ask. Reach out. Be an
> answer to some one's plea. You have a part to play.
> Have faith. We can decide to risk that He is indeed
> there, watching, caring, cherishing us as we love and
> accept love. The world will be a better place for it.
> And wherever they are, the angels will dance."
>
> —JOAN WESTER ANDERSON

Angel Ishmael

What Is Paradise?

I am one of three Angels to speak today. According to some men, we do not exist, but according to most of the world, we do. Why is it that man has such a difficult time believing in Angels? It is because they are not yet ready for something other than themselves. Do you want a clear picture of faith? It is like hang gliding in the air, knowing the wind will catch your sails and you will glide. Complete, pure faith is like turning loose of the safe ground. Will your faith be enough to hold you safely in the air, or will you fear and fall? Faith is taking a step, not sure of where the path is going but knowing that is the way. Many, many times your Spirit will ask you to leap, jump, let go, and every time you go through these tests, your faith will grow. Your faith is what will "save" you and make you whole. So, then, if you believe God created all beings, and we are even listed in the Bible, why then do you doubt? Do you doubt because you fear? Why do you fear? Because you have not found the truth! The truth of your existence and the truth of ours.

From the beginning, we have existed, just like you. Oh, yes, you were there. Your Spirit existed as a part of God. When the decision was made that the whole should expand and burst out as extensions, you became you, yet still a part of God. You are made in God's image. But what part of you? Your Spirit. In other words, you are Source! Now when you incarnate, we accompany you by leading, guiding, protecting, and encouraging. We are the thoughts of God. Do you see? You are not separate or alone. Never! If you think you are, it is just a façade of which you have convinced yourself. In other words, you have shut your eyes and said no one is there. Yet, you are totally surrounded! We just wait on you to see the truth, the light.

Never before have we seen humans want to open their eyes as now. The ones who do not believe will tell you all their fears so that they do not have to believe in anything other than themselves. They essentially do not want to go through the process of having more faith. The world is crying out to God, and God is responding, but not the way so many have imagined. You see, God is also the Great Teacher. Your soul has to learn. So, when you pray for peace on Earth, sometimes tidal waves roll and the ground quakes. People are stretched to their farthest limits, and their souls begin to learn. Every day God will teach you something new, but how many of you want to learn? Do you hunger and thirst for it? You should know that knowledge and wisdom lead to enlightenment. Enlightenment leads to paradise. What is paradise? It is fully being in complete awareness of the whole body of God.

Who you are and what everything else is. Instead of having one piece of the pie, you have the whole pie or understanding. Sometimes in your existence, someone tries very hard to give you another piece of the pie, but so many of you do not want it. Why? Because this means you would have to change. Change from what? A false sense of truth or existence. An example would be if the Church of Christ looked at the Baptist and said they were going to Hell because they didn't have the appropriate way. You see what you have done is take the whole big picture or nugget of gold and sliced a little chunk off and said, "This is all there is." How falsely you are speaking!

Woe to you to judge another's path that God has created. Yes, I said *God*! Everything good and bad, light and dark, comes from God. God only uses the dark to help you see the light or the truth. You actually use it the same way, but many of you get lost in the darkness and forget the light. That is why I am here, giving you this message today, to encourage you to see the whole. Don't hold on to your little piece and live in untruth. Ask God to help you see the whole, so that you will begin the steps to paradise. Knowledge, wisdom, and enlightenment equals Paradise. Make sure at each step you do not say that this is all there is. Don't get stuck in a comfortable place; keep growing. Woe to you who hears but does not receive. For your judgment or lesson becomes greater. Open your hearts and begin to trust. There is more than Shamanism. There is more than Catholicism. There is more than Protestantism. There is so much more . . . Amen.

I see a female Angel, small, yet sweet, holding a single pink rose in her right hand. In her left hand, blood runs from her palm. Yet, she smiles gently, and with much precision, she lays the blossom of the rose on the ground. Light emanates from her hands, and the wounds disappear. The Angel's lesson is this:

The rose represents truth. It can often be a beautiful rose, yet it has thorns. The thorns are used to pierce the darkness or the untruth of what we have created. Hence in the left hand, the blood runs. This is the emotion, but just as the thorns have pierced, the same element will heal if we choose to allow it. We all have the light within ourselves to heal ourselves, but do we want to?

It is hard to imagine that God would create light and dark, rose blossom and the thorns on the same element. Yet, they are so useful. There was no mistake. For God doesn't make mistakes. Do not fear the thorns of your life. For they are used to teach you many things. Learn to heal yourself. Do not wait for another. The light remains within you. The rose is in your hand. You lack nothing. Learn from the bleeding. The bleeding shows you who you really are—separate in the body, but a whole with all of existence. Blessed are you, for you have just received the blessing of peace. Peace I leave with you, and peace you will find within yourselves. May you be truly understood within yourself. Amen.

> *"To love for the sake of being loved is human,*
> *but to love for the sake of loving is angelic."*
>
> —ALPHONSE DE LAMARTINE

Archangel Raphael

What Is It That You Are Creating in Your Life?

How many of you today, if you could, would heal yourself? What does it mean to heal? Healing means understanding, then releasing, then balancing. It's a three-step process. It sounds very easy, but sometimes it is not. Now that you know what healing is, will you allow yourself to do it? Many of you will sit and stir the pot, never having the thought of letting the food or emotion be done. Why is it that when you cook food, you have a timer and do not overcook it? But when you have emotions, you never stop cooking and stirring! Why is this? Why do you want to stay at the pot? It is because somehow it fills you, but you begin to lose much of the world around you since you never leave the pot! I challenge you today: if you are stirring an emotion that you cannot let go of or leave behind, please hand the spoon to God! God is the master taste-tester. He/She will tell you if your food or emotion is worth keeping, and then God can dispose of it for you. You can heal! You just

85

have to want to. I, myself, would choose healing, because if you can have the light of letting go, why would you want the darkness of holding on? These things are really very simple. You just have to make steps. You just have to decide.

As Angel Ariel said, why not use all the colors or emotions instead of only using one? The only reason why humans hold on is because they are scared they will not feel anything else again. How silly is that? Here is an example: you are married and your spouse passes over. You weep and mourn. This is okay until you never leave your mourning and weeping state. You refuse joy, laughter, happiness, and growth because you are unsure they will be there. You do not trust God! So, you stay at your pot, stirring these emotions and never going anywhere else. Do you see? You are in control, and you are deciding what you will allow yourself to feel. No one or God is making you feel any other way. This is part of your free will down here.

No one makes you feel any certain way! You choose it. You are responsible for your feelings. No one adds food to your pot; no one takes it out, only you. If there is an emotion today that you are feeling, stop blaming it on someone else. Take responsibility for your emotions and simply decide if they are worth holding on to. If they are not, ask God to help you throw them out so you can put in your pot the emotion that you choose. No one is to blame because you make the choices! When you realize that you make the choices, then you become empowered to heal your life. God, the Angels, and all of the Spirit world are here to guide, love, and help you. In taking responsibility for your life and your emotions, you begin to see your true form. Your true form is that you are a piece of the Creator. I ask you today, what is it that you are creating in your life? Amen.

Angel Pealise
(The Angel of Laughter)

Just Become Joyful

Why have I come today? To signify change. Change of what? Change or the choice of the body chemistry. Do you know that when you laugh, all the circuits in your body light up and connect? Did you know that when you laugh, your immune system rises to unbelievable levels? Did you know that when you laugh, black soot falls and melts away like powder from your auric body. Did you know that God created laughter?

If you know God, even a little bit, then you will know that God creates everything for a purpose and a power. So then, why don't you laugh more? Just become joyful! Pure laughter, pure joy heals all wounds. Not laughter that is making fun at someone else's expense, or laughter that comes from or causes destruction. Pure laughter and pure joy. This heals. This reconnects you to the very Source that you are. You humans are creatures of habit. Why not make a habit once a day to laugh? Really laugh and find your joy. If you do, your stress will leave, your mind will ease itself, your body will heal, and you will be a joy to be around.

People who usually attract other people like magnets generally laugh a lot. I have been given as much laughter to hand out as you humans will use. It's like the gold fairy dust, and it is also spreadable from one of you to the next. Have you ever got lost in someone else's laughter? Then, before you know it, you were laughing? Laughter is the best medicine. It can touch you where nothing else can. I have as much as you will ever need. Try it. Blessed are those who mourn, for they shall be comforted, loved, and filled with the joy of the living God. Blessed are you who read this today, for I truly say that pure laughter is a powerful medicine and a wonderful gift. Amen.

For I see a vision of an angel riding a monster with five horns. The horns are the fear, dread, worry, jealousy, and greed. The monster embodies the power of these atrocities. The Angel has harnessed these energies and rides the monster as she swings her golden dust of laughter. Fear, dread, worry, jealousy, and greed fall off as pebbles, and the monster turns into a butterfly—for the Angel has transformed me from a monster to a monarch. Thanks be to God. Amen.

Angel Ariel

Today Is a Blank Canvas; Create as You Wish

Today may seem as just another day to you, but really it is so much more than that. Yesterday has come and gone, and tomorrow will do the same. But today is today. It is a blank canvas ready for you to create as you wish, yet many of you will let others create it for you. You have been given many colors from which to choose for your painting. Some of you choose only red, the color of passion. It can help you create amazing things, or it can take you to levels of energy that are much too high for you. This results in anger, rage, or lust, etc. . . . Some of you choose orange. Orange is the color of a large fountain—a communal fountain from which everyone can drink from the orange water of community.

Some of you would drink just enough to be satisfied, and some of you will continue to drink until you make yourself sick. You have too much community, and do not have the balance of being alone/solitude. Some of you choose yellow. You wear it like a badge; this is your strength. Yet some of you have a noticeable, and yet perfect size, but some of you have a badge so large it covers or blocks your view of where you are going. You lose sight. Some of you choose pink. Some of you eat the pink cotton candy and are satisfied, yet some of you cannot get enough. You grow sad and forget that the vendor (God) always makes enough cotton candy (love), and you cry. Some of you choose blue. Many of you will paint your blue or communicate and be done, but many of you paint so much blue that no one wants to see your blue or listen to you speak so much. You need stillness and peace. Some of you will paint indigo. You will use it like a radio, speaking with the main communications center. But some of you will use it so much that you burn up the system. Some of you will paint with white and gold. You will use as much as you want, and it is never too much. But some of you will only use a small amount and will be therefore lacking greatly in the connection with the Source. You see, it is about balance.

My message today is about balance. Instead of getting stuck on one color today and taking it to an extreme, why don't you try to use all of the colors to paint your portrait. You are the artist. It will be as you paint it to be. Do you not see that God uses all of the colors of this world? The sky is blue, and the grass is green. Each day ask yourself how you are balancing your world. Use all of the colors God has given you to make your rainbows. When you embody all that is, then you will begin to become whole. For those of you reading this book, I ask that God will open your eyes so that you may see all of the possibilities that lie before you. You are limitless and full . . .

Angel Mariah

I Am in My Father, and You in Me, and I in You

Do not look outside of you, but look within you to know all the answers. Simple isn't it? Do you know what makes a person tick—*tick* meaning to "run" or continue the body with the soul with the Spirit? It is their will. Today, we are going to talk about the will and why you have it. Many see the will as determination, strength, hope, and/or stubbornness, but I will tell you the truth of the will. See, your bodies are lined up: physical body, soul body, spiritual body. Now, the will is a gold cord or thread or substance that weaves through all of the bodies and connects them together. Sometimes when people become disenchanted with their life, sick without a diagnosis, or possessed by evil, it is because their golden will has come undone or unattached to one of the bodies. They feel disconnected. If this continues, then they will want to escape as in suicide or just leave what they know, or they simply die from whatever disease comes along. Now, did you know that you can willingly untie the will and let your self expire without any suffering?

The difference is you, not a trauma or fear, untied the will. What unties the will determines how the bodies will separate out. For example, when an older person says, "I am tired and I am ready to go home to heaven," they may simply lie down in their bed and in their sleep, untie the will and slip out. You see, the difference is awareness. God said, "My people are perishing for lack of knowledge," and this is why I am telling you this. Do not perish, but live. Even in the dying of your physical body, if you are aware of this, then you will never perish. So, how do you see where your will is? You do a system check. Just as you would on a car or anything else. Close your eyes. Stay there until nothing else is in your thoughts. Now, address the bodies as if you were addressing (very gently) employees. Ask them to show the standing of your will from your physical body to your spiritual body.

Your will should spiral all the way up and down, connecting all three bodies. When it does make a loop or twist, it should wrap around all three bodies. If it does not loop around all three bodies, then there is your faulty connection. You are a bit like an electrician finding the loss of electricity or contact. Now, ask to see what caused the disconnection. When one of the bodies finishes telling you, then you ask this disconnection to simply leave. Reconnect the memory of yourself by asking the Holy Spirit to come and connect you and you will be whole again.

Jesus said, "And I will pray to the Father, and he will give you another helper who may abide with you forever—the Spirit of truth, whom the world cannot receive, because it neither sees Him nor knows Him. For He dwells with you and will be in you. At that day you will know that I am in My Father, and you in Me, and I in you." John 14:16–17, 20.

Jesus healed, cured, exorcised, and raised from the dead because he knew of the golden cord of will, and he simply reconnected it through the purest channeled form of God. When Jesus left, he said, "But the Helper, the Holy Spirit, whom the Father will send in my name. He will teach you all things, and bring to your remembrance all things that I said to you." John 14:26.

So, now you should ask these tasks to be performed by the Holy Spirit. Do you understand that the Holy Spirit is the "master electrician"? Everything God created has a purpose. This is one of the purposes for the Holy Spirit. It serves as a very, very powerful Source of love and healing. Do not reconnect others or yourselves out of fear, but out of love only. When you can understand and know this, then you can perform what you deem as miracles. Amen.

"They will come from the bright, sunny land,
Come on their pinions so fair;
Jesus will send them its glory to tell,
Angels will carry me there."

—FANNY CROSBY, WILL THE ANGELS COME?

Apostle Mark

The World Is but a Movie

Today, we will cover a large territory, so open your mind to the idea of vastness and authority. I am referring to the option you have in your life. Every day, you awaken, and from your first sight, you begin to decide. As you do this, you also decide who and what will affect you and how it will impact your life. Also, you must realize what you want. Why do you crave this or that? What are you trying to fill or see within? The first place to start is your eyes. You choose to see what you want. You become witness to everything you turn your eyes to. Then you begin to interpret your world. It feels good, it feels bad. It is less, it is too much. You see, what you see you draw conclusions from. You see, you need to be aware of where you are putting your focus in this life. No one made you focus on any one thing. This is of your own choosing, or what God likes to refer to as your free will.

Now, what if I told you that what you see is like an outdoor drive-in movie screen. You are watching, but the one mistake you make is that you get so lost in the movie that you forget you are separate from it. You are only watching, and it is not reality! You exist outside the movie because you are real. Your world is like the movie, but only realize that the Source is where reality and non-reality come from. You are not the movie. It is being shown to you, but it is not real.

Reality is what lies around this life. This is why we urge

all of you to meditate. Close your eyes and see truth, reality. No one can make you. This you have to do on your own. Now, let's go deeper. If you had your choice, and you do, what movie would you go to the drive-in to see? *Forrest Gump, Steel Magnolias, Armageddon, Top Gun, Lorenzo's Oil,* or maybe nothing. Yes, nothing. There are some who come down and evolve so quickly that they shut their eyes and refuse the movie screen. It becomes blank, and they begin to see reality. Reality of existence, of their existence, and more.

So whom do you most admire and wish to be? Perhaps it's the actors, actresses, the people who serve at the drive-in or just the movie-goer? You see, you have to know that what you are looking at in this life you purchased the ticket to see. No one made you.

Do you need to know any more on this subject? Hopefully not. You have just received a great piece of advice. Be present, but always choose the movie screen you really want to see. Sometimes, mostly all the time, it is when our screen is empty that we see the most! Blessed are you who have received the word and not just heard but understood. May all of your days be days of complete existence. Always knowing who you are! God Speed. Amen.

> *"The angels are as perfect in form as they are in spirit."*
> —JEANNE D'ARC

Angel Razchiel

You Are a Masterpiece of God

Do not look so forlorn about your ascension back into the heavens. For you are but a water droplet descended upon the Earth, and you will evaporate to ascend back from where you came. There is no mistake for your presence on the Earth and no mistake of your ascent. Blessed are you who knows who and what you are. For in this you realize you are made right and beautiful—full of the Glory of the One True God, full of goodness and praise within yourself. You are the descension and ascension of the "Raining God."

From the heavens to the Earth and from the Earth back to the heavens, both are blessed to receive you and your goodness. All of your days are spent cycling for the One True God. Holy are you who know your place, for you give life to the Earth and life you bring to all the heavens. Beautiful is your descent and glorious is your return home—home to where there is only all that is. Glorious and right are your actions in falling and rising up. Hereafter, you will not hide your face but will choose to see what is real: that you were created a wonderful masterpiece of God, and that is all there is to be. Amen.

> *"We shall find peace. We shall hear angels,*
> *we shall see the sky sparkling with diamonds."*
> —ANTON CHEKHOV

Spirit of Truth, The Golden Light

You Are My Light;
You Are Part of Me

Author's observation: There appears to be golden light all around the room. Brighter than the sun. Glorious as what it is reflecting . . . God.

No two creations are exactly the same, and I have made you so for a sure purpose. I did not intend for all of you to be alike or you would never completely experience all that I would have you to experience. I know you. I know you, and there is nothing you can ever do to make me not know you. You can change your shape, your hair color, your weight, your heart, your mind, but I still know you, and you are a part of me. Today may have been an unexpected day, a sad day, a normal day, or a joyful day, but I am still knowing you. In all of your emotions and thoughts, I still know you. You have not changed even so much that your creator cannot recognize or distinguish you.

I wait for you to recognize me. I never change. I am all that there is. I often thought that this would make things easier on you to find me this way. The truth is, your true self never changes. Your real self. The real body I gave you. It just gets brighter and brighter. No matter how many mistakes or pain your soul creates for your body, your spiritual light, your true self never fades. Because it is me. I will always be you and within you. It is the other layers that get worn or threadbare or tired. Time has a way of doing this to everything that houses Spirit unless directed otherwise. Yes, I said *directed otherwise*. Do you not think that if it is your plan to live two hundred fifty years your body can and will as long as all of your wills are lined up together in harmony? Or even after your soul has left the body, if we will for it to be preserved for a purpose, do you not think that it will? See, you and I are the same. Always connected; always the same.

We remain. We simply remain. I want you to know that I love you. You are my light. You are parts of me. I cannot exist without all of you existing, because we are one. There is no separation. A Spirit, a light, cannot go to Hell nor can it be contained. Why is it that the human form wants to contain it? Maybe because it itself is a container to house the Spirit. But Spirit cannot be completely housed. For it is connected to everything. Your human form cannot keep it from connecting. It would be like telling a particle of water in the ocean not to touch the other particles and to stay in one place. Silly, isn't it? Do you see, there is no separation, no ending, only existing. You and I just are. When you accept this, you will see that you, the real you, is wonderfully made. Amen.

> *"If you seek an angel with an open heart . . .*
> *You shall always find one."*
>
> —Anonymous

Disciple John

Are You the Fisherman or the Pole?

What is rejection? It is God's way of putting you (the soul or body) on the correct path you had chosen. God will always direct your path if you acknowledge God. All it takes is a thought, word, or action toward God, and it can be done. We have to all feel the sting of rejection, not being "let in," but in reality, we should not want to be "let in." We should "want out"—out to the things that are pure. For in that pureness, there is no rejection. Being "out" means to be directed to the purest place of existence, and when you come to that place, there is peace, love, and acceptance. Humans are so busy wanting in, wanting there, and being contained that they forget there is no container to Spirit. It simply is. It penetrates, goes through, permeates, migrates, and floats through everything. It is lighter than air and more fluid than water. It is the purest essence, one that can hardly be described through words, but only by experience or memory.

You have existed since there was existence, so why would you expect or relate to rejection? It is only felt and stored in the body and the soul. Nowhere else! Your light body, your true self, does not store negative! Your Spirit is like water that cannot be contained and never dries up. Do you see? Do not be so bogged down in your senses. For what you sense is your soul/body. Why don't you try to sense your Spirit/light body? That is the real part of you anyway. Your Spirit is like a fisherman. The pole and string are your soul. The bobber and bait are your mind and emotion. The water is your body. You see, you can get reeled in, thrown out, tossed about, but the real you is not just that; it is the fisherman. The fisherman is the Spirit that decides where the other parts are to go and move.

When you feel out of control, unsure, unsteady, insecure, rejected, and uncomfortable, it is because you think or have identified with the pole, string, bobber, or bait. Go back to your true self, the fisherman. Steady yourself in the truth. You are all fishermen of God. Steadying your pole, trying to "catch an experience" in this life. Come back home, back to where you really are. John 3:16: "For God so loved the world (Earth, creation) that he gave his only begotten Son (you and me, Spirit body in earthly body) that whosoever (soul) believeth in Him (the Spirit, our true self) shall not perish (soul: feel pain, misery, sorrow) but have everlasting life (you know then that you will endure, exist forever). Just as Jesus rose, so shall you. Just as Jesus knew, so can you. Just as Jesus healed, so can you. Jesus was the example. Jesus was to lead you to your true self; therefore, saving you from untruth, which begot pain and sorrow. Jesus was the Messiah, Savior of ignorance. He is God, but so are you! Jesus just knew it, and you didn't until now.

Don't you see? Let Christ be the teacher to open your eyes. See who you are—an only begotten child of God, who too has a purpose. Blessed are you who have worshipped but not seen the truth. The truth is in you—you/Spirit/Kingdom of God/light body. Oh, blessed be you who have come searching, for you shall be filled with righteousness so full that your ears will forever hear the angelic voices and the choir of God. Holy and immaculate are you. Perfect and right in your creation. Do not make what God created any less than just that. You are sons and daughters of God. Now you know your name. Blessed be. Blessed be all those who hear and understand. Blessed be. Amen. All Glory to God.

God/Holy Spirit
Archangels
Powers Principalities
Virtues Seraphim
Cherubim Guardians
Messengers Deities
Nature Spirits Plants, Rocks, Animal Spirits
Sons and Daughters (Us)

The Holy Spirit holds the truth of who you are. You are washed in the Holy Spirit, then you ascend home. Holy Spirit guides, heals, leads, blesses. It descends on you like rain. It changes your physical and soul body forever. Your souls are all striving to be as Jesus. Aware, knowing completely, evolved. God made Jesus' earthly body perfect. His mental body, emotional body, and soul body were perfect so that perfection and complete awareness always existed.

"I saw the tracks of angels in the earth:
the beauty of heaven walking by itself on the world."
—PETRARCH

Angel Saphron

There Is No Such Thing
as Disconnection from God

Today, we are going to discuss telling the truth and why it is so important to your life path. First, your life path is only based on truth, and truth is God. When you refuse to see or understand or speak the truth, you begin to move off the path that has been set in front of you. When you move off your soul path, you begin to lose sight of what is real in existence and what is not. Many of you lie to yourselves. It could be as simple as "I am not good enough," or it could be complex and involve others: "I am not in love with him because it cannot work." Do you understand that a lie removes you from a soul path that has been planned for you? You are not who you think you are. You are Krishna, destroying and creating as you go. Do you not seek nirvana? Then look within yourselves.

All of your lives you are told to "walk a certain way, carry a certain look, be a certain way," but, in reality, all you are to do is walk your path. You cannot do this if you lie to yourself

103

and live in denial of all there is to be done. How many of you today know the next step? How many of you are uncertain of the next step? When you become uncertain, instead of trying to make yourself feel better, you should ask God what is the next step and that God gives you the strength to uphold that truthful walk. When you lie to yourself and others, you are not trusting God and you are trying to disconnect from Source.

I would like to tell you that there is no such thing as disconnection from God or Source. You can put your hands over your eyes, but God is still seeing you. This you need to realize and make peace with. Did you know God already planned your path for you and God is already there? If God is already there tomorrow, in two years, or two hundred years, then what are you so afraid of? When you do not trust your innermost self, your Spirit/light body, then you do not trust God. Be quiet, be still, and breathe the breath of God. Why do you think Jesus meditated? It was to keep himself in total and complete alignment with the will of God, which happened to be the will or agreement of his Spirit and soul path. If Jesus did not connect within himself, and if Jesus did not trust God, then do you really think that he would have let them capture him, torture him, and crucify him? Come on. Now are you beginning to understand?

If you want to walk the path, the path you chose, then stay connected on a conscious and subconscious level. All you need to know is within you—your plans, your trials, your triumphs, your joys. When you are meant to know, they will reveal themselves to you. Now, this brings us to another topic, timing. Everything has a special purpose and time. That is the law of this world. God tried to tell you that in Ecclesiastes chapter 3:1–8,11: "To everything there is a season, a time for every purpose under Heaven; a time to be born, and a time to die; a time to plant, and a time to pluck what is planted; a time to kill, and a time to heal; a time to break down, and a time to build up; a time to weep, and a time to laugh; a time to mourn, a time to dance; a time to cast away stones, and a time to gather stones; a time to embrace, and a time to refrain from embracing; a time to gain, and a time to lose: a time to keep, and a time to throw away: a time to tear, and a time to sew: a time to keep silence, and a time to speak: a time to love, and a time to hate: a time of war, and a time of peace. He has made everything beautiful in its time. Also He has put eternity in their hearts, except that no one can find out the work that God does from beginning to end."

Timing is imperative, and if you rush things and not let them happen in their natural order, there will be consequences of this. For example, if a doctor induced a pregnant mother at six months of gestation, the baby would come too early and all the consequences and struggles would come to formation. What is it that makes you rush about so much? Why don't you trust God enough to let God induce the "birth," and why is it that you are frightened of pain? Don't you know that pain is just in the soul/physical bodies? It does not exist in the Spirit form. The Spirit is pure water that cannot be contaminated.

Don't you see that everything has its place in time? Rome was not built in one day and neither were the pyramids. It is the process that made Rome and Egypt strong. Not the buildings, temples, or pyramids they built. They learned, worked together, encouraged, dreamed, laughed, cried, and died together for this purpose. That is the most important part, not the structures they left. They are just a reflection of the endurance of these souls' journey. Sometimes the very most important things in life are those you cannot see with the physical eyes, but are the experiences and feelings that you have.

Do you understand that in order to stay in your body, the body, mind, heart, and soul must feel in order to stay connected to one another? If you were to will all your feelings from yourself completely, you would slip out of your bodies as a helium balloon slipping from a child's hands. It would be that easy. Now, this brings us to our next topic, which is feelings. Did you know that God made you to feel? If you did not feel, then you would stop moving on your path. What sense do you use to walk down your path? Is it sight? Can you see visions, glimpses, or signs or lights to show you the way? Do you hear? Is there some Spirit, God-force that whispers to you, instructs you as to where to go? Do you touch energy or matter? Does everything have to be felt ("It just feels right") for you to know? Or do you just ask for the right light to manifest, not having to use your senses but just waiting for God to manifest and appear?

There are many ways to hear or know the path. Do not take for granted your experience here. This is a large part of God, and together you create and form life itself. Do you see that you are loved? Not the way you know love, but real love. Don't you see this is what all of your physical/soul bodies want: the real love? God. Open your hearts and minds today. Ask God to show you a better way to live. Walk the soul path you were meant for and stop lying to yourself. You are blessed, you are whole, and you are loved. You are God, and God is you (Spirit body). Amen.

"Angels don't worry about you. . . .
They believe in you."

—ANONYMOUS

Angels Malachi and Neoriam

Darkness Is a Time of Growth

Greetings. Today we are going to talk about cost. The cost of everything that you see, how you hear, and at times, how you understand. Whenever you relish in the things that God has made, there will never be a cost. *Cost* just means that a price had to be paid for the buying or exchanging of that particular experience or enjoyment. Did you know that when you are buying the things that belong to God's Spirit that all is free? Some of these things are love, life, freedom, joy, sorrow, pain, and loss. Quite surprised are you that there are negatives in the items listed that are free? Well, you shouldn't be.

Who do you think made the darkness, and who do you think made the light? If you say not the same person or creator, then you are wrong! When you say God, Creator, we say that all things come from this. The Lord of all, overseer, Creator of all that is. Do not forget that you too helped in creation, for in Genesis 1:26, God said, "Let Us make Man in Our image, according to our likeness." Let's just say that you had a hand in all things that are good. Negative emotion can be very good because it brings you back to your center! When things are always easy or always good, the physical body/soul body forgets about the Spirit and does not let it direct the course.

When the negative emotions are felt, it is so that these bodies can turn to Spirit and put the Master Creator back in charge. Compassion is knowing that there is something greater than your physical body and giving love to it. Did you know that without negative emotion, you would have no peace here on the Earth plane? The light is the light because it shines against the darkness, and the darkness is the darkness because it stands against the light. Both are part of God's plan. Did you know that in the beginning God brought light into darkness? Genesis 1:1–5 says, "In the beginning God (you and God) created the Heaven and the Earth. The Earth was without form and void: and darkness was on the face of the deep. And the Spirit of God was hovering over the face of the waters. Then God said, 'Let there be light,' and there was light. And God saw the light, that it was good; and God divided the light from the darkness. God called the light day, and the darkness He called night. So that the beginning and morning were the first day." Now, do you see that both are of God? God is above, beyond light and dark but not of it. Now what about Satan, you ask, and all of his legions?

This happens to be another category, and story we will explain later. The other thing that we came to talk about is why you fear the darkness? Did you know that darkness is a time for resting, recuperation, and regrouping? It is also a time of growth. Think about an unborn child. God did not light up the inside of the womb but left it dark for many reasons. You see there was a plan, there is a plan, and there will always be a plan according to God. How many of you know when you close your eyes there is darkness? Do you think God created your eyelids for a purpose? Why then do you assume then that darkness is evil or bad?

Let me tell you this. Evil or bad is represented by Satan, and Satan can appear cloaked in the darkness or the light. He is a master of disguise and quite good at what he does. This is why the Bible says to "be aware of a wolf in sheep's clothing." Satan is a master teacher and embodies the opposite of God. God is love; Satan is not. God is good; Satan is evil. God is work and creation—life; Satan is destruction. God is secure; Satan takes your sanity, your security, and your hope. You need to be aware of what things are and how to judge them. Jesus said you have eyes to see, but you do not see. You have ears to hear, but you do not hear. We are here to help you see and hear. Philippians 2:5–6 says, "Let this mind be in you that was also in Christ Jesus, who, being in the form of God, did not consider it robbery to be equal with God." (Jesus was the man but Christ was the consciousness.)

Did you know that there are numerous reasons why God allows Satan to exist? Did you know that God has made a vow with Satan, and that there is a time limit to this world? Did you know that the only thing that can change darkness and create God more on this plane is love? Did you know that when you love, you are doing the works of God? You are living the light-God that you are. You are all sparkles, fragments of the One True God. You just have to know this. Philippians 2:13 says, "For it is God who works in you both to will and to do for His good pleasure." Now, are you understanding the three points?: God and Us, Light and Dark-Creation, and Satan or destruction and death. Did you know that when you descend down, you die? You have to go through destruction of the physical body, and then you ascend to God. Why do you think it says that Jesus had overcome death and holds the keys to Hell? Revelation:1:18 says, "I am He who lives, and was dead, and behold, I am alive forever more, And I have the keys of Hades and of death."

It is because things greatly shifted when Jesus descended and created the life he created. He changed the main contract between God and Satan. Instead of a place of abandonment, loss, and forlornness, now Hell is just a passing-through to get from one plane to another. Before, if the soul were not living in awareness of Spirit and had "forgotten" it would pass into Hell and stay there until it could understand and remember. Then the soul would ascend. But when Jesus came, taught, was crucified and died, he changed the rules. Now, when you die, of course, you pass through, but you do not stay because you have "forgotten God"; your soul stays only out of your own choosing.

Hell is not as nearly as full as before. Jesus came to reteach who you really are on all levels, and the Bible was constructed so that you should remember who you are. Here is the only dilemma in this: how many of you are choosing Hell and why? Did you know it is an empty place of abandonment and fear? Did you know you are choosing this out of wrong knowledge or simply out of guilt? Did you know that, for some, it is easier to "hide" in Hell from God than it is to face God, work a new plan, reincarnate, and correct or balance the actions and emotions of the previous life? Jesus said, "Do not fear, only believe."

Believe means to know or become familiar with on all levels. Fear is empty and hollow like a dark hole or a pit that sucks in all things that are good and right. How many of you spend your day in fear rather than in belief? Did you know that God did not directly create fear? Satan formed fear and uses it like balls of destruction, pounding you on all corners. Did you know that, for some time now, you have all feared who you really are? If you really see who you are and know that Satan has no power over you, then Satan would no longer exist. Why do you think Satan throws balls of fear at the churches and the people? If he can keep you confused and judging and condemning one another, then you will never figure it out, and he will continue to exist. Interesting, isn't it? So then we have come to help you understand. Step boldly into the mirror of God, see yourself and all that you are, rebuke fear and emptiness, and come into a life full of the blessings of God. To God be all the Glory and upon us may His Grace descend like merciful drops of rain cleansing away our ignorance and replenishing us with power and authority. Amen.

> *"Both angels and demons are ignorant of the future, yet they make predictions. The angels do so when God reveals the future to them and commands them to prophesy, and what they prophesy comes to pass. Demons also make predictions, but these are only guesses based on what they see from afar."*
>
> —JOHN OF DAMASCUS

Angel Starinia

The Colors of Sex

Hello. Today I greet you with a new understanding of the act of sex, consummating yourselves with one another. I want to discuss with you what happens and why God created this act. For two to come together symbolizes such a powerful act that it can never be undone by man. The actual act symbolizes a merging of many levels, levels that cannot be seen with the eyes. Let us now talk about these levels. The first level is spiritual. Many people commit this physical act and the Spirits never merge. This is the difference between what humans call making love and sex. When you make love with another, the Spirits touch and merge, depending on the soul plan and the depth of love between the two. Actually, this act of merging Spirits is very beautiful to us. We see this in colors and lights.

The two merge and shine so bright or they touch and light up like a firefly against the darkness. This act is what you say is "blessed by God" because of spiritual touching.

Now, the next level is the souls connecting. This, too, is very powerful because of karma, past lives, and soul knowledge. Somehow you are a familiar to one another. Somehow you can read one another. You know what the other wants, and you do not have to speak it. This can be seen by humans through the eyes. Yes, the eyes are the windows to the soul. When souls touch, there is such a powerful connection that it literally creates energetic sparks. Here is where passion and love are felt on the same plane. Very few people know this plane. They reside so often in the other four planes that they rarely find this level. When two people do, you can hardly keep them apart. They tend to be consumed with one another and have a language all of their own. This is where soul mates are born. So many souls want this experience, but not every soul gets this in every lifetime. When these two converge and life's plan tends to pull them apart, they never quite get over it.

These are the mourners and grievers in society, and nothing else in this world compares with the spark or flame. Everything pales in comparison. This can be very devastating to the soul, and this is why not every soul is aloud this experience again and again in every incarnation. Now, the next level is mental converging. Here in this plane is where two people become like business partners. When minds converge, they work side by side, and nothing seems too big or too large for them to tackle. When this happens, we see a soft blue-violet flame ignite and burn slow. You will not always agree, but you will always work together to form your life path. This

is a powerful combination, and many people diagnose or give this the phrase "We are on the same page" or "We connected and had so much in common" or "We both want the same things." You see, desire and foresight start in the mind so that this connection yields good homes, businesses, and material possessions if the two are in a positive cycle.

The next plane of connection is emotional, and this area can get confusing and sticky. The heart holds many different needs, hurts, joys, memories, and fears. Two can connect here because they have a need to be filled and the other seems to fill it. For example, consider a woman had an absent father at times in her life so she chooses a mate that seems like her father so that the void can be filled. Here is another example: a man had an abusive mother so he connects his heart to a woman who is nurturing, healing, and gentle. Do you see that many people connect at the heart but that few relationships last here? It feels safe for a while, but at some point, the one who is being filled the most gets antsy and needs a change or more out of their mate. This is because you have to fix your own wounds! Patient heal thyself! Healing is within you, not without you.

You are the one who gives permission to heal or not. These relationships usually are the ones that end up in counseling and have a fifty-fifty chance of survival, depending, of course, on their life path. This connection looks like a sparkler going off—a very soft pink to a red color sometimes mixed with purple. It is a nice glow, but it just sometimes does not last. These relationships begin to feel more like friendship or brother-sister relationship.

The last plane of connection is physical, and when that is all that is connecting, this is what you label as just sex. So many or all the time when it is only sex, it is merely instinctual and biological. It could feel very passionate, but in reality, the body chemistries just perfectly match up, and it could feel very explosive. This is where pheromones, looks, and tastes are deciding factors. "He smelled amazing." or "Did you *see* her?" Many times, when this act is formed, we see a green color—all shades to a yellow. Many times, if this is the only place of connection, you will feel empty inside because all the other planes simply did not get to connect. Many people feel guilty and never really understand how or why they let this happen. They interpret this as their heart plane saying, "You don't even know him and you certainly don't love or feel love with him." The mind may say, "How could you rationally commit this act? Goodness only knows what you could have gotten or how are you are going to forgive yourself."

The soul may say, "I feel empty and embarrassed. I never connected and don't really want to." The Spirit may be interpreted as saying, "This was adultery/fornication. How could you?" But, in reality, you are only feeling every plane telling you it did not connect, and it wanted to. This does not feel good. You humans are the ones who form the words from the other planes. They are just giving you the sensation of not being able to connect.

Now, when two come together, only one or many more planes will connect, depending on choice and soul plan. For example, it could be that you choose a partner in which the physical, heart, and mind planes connect. You learn, fill one another, and correct karma, and when it is over, it is over. You have failed at nothing. The path just ran its course and you have come to an end. Let it be, and release each other with love, please!

Some forms come together and have physical, heart, mind, and soul. This is a powerful connection, and these usually are the ones who, after their spouse passes over, they pass on very soon also, or they seem to live the rest of their life in grief and sorrow. Most usually die soon after their mate.

It is possible to connect all five, and when this happens,

it is like a fireworks show to us. You float. You reach heights of ecstasy never before felt or were aware of. You are full, brimming over the edges. You have all of the levels connecting, and rarely do these individuals separate. They seem to fit and have a perfect balance because it is the Spirit connection that balances all the other planes. This is why preachers say, "What God has joined together, let no man separate." You see, when the Spirits are joined, and you and God worked this into the plan, then no man can separate this. But not every marriage God ordains and not every couple connects at the Spirit level. It is because you are not supposed to.

You should not feel guilty in not connecting but should just learn to pay very close attention to what God is instructing you to do for your souls' path. Do you understand? Forgive yourselves, learn your plan, ask for instructions, and go forward. God told you there would be a time to laugh and a time to cry, a time to build up and a time to tear down, and a time to live and a time to die. You are supposed to experience all of these things. Guilt was created to let you know that you are or were not following your souls' path. Stop, drop and pray, ask for directions and get back on track. When you do this peace will come. Even if you feel you should divorce or split or leave, if it is your Souls" path directed by God you will have peace within. Now, let us talk about other Souls, babies who are born into these connections.

They are usually born to enhance the souls' plan and either connect or disconnect the two who have consummated, depending on the plan. Sometimes they are born to separate them, but keep them connected on a physical plan to learn compassion and forgiveness of each other. This has many layers, and we will discuss this further down, but the main point I am trying to make is, you were born to your parents to either enhance or tear down what was there. Let go of your responsibility, because just by being born, you did fulfill the greater purpose. Why do you think babies cannot talk? Because the plan would never go through. The baby would tell all. Remember, your parents had their own plans. You did your job by being born, now let go of your parents' karma and lessons. They are not yours to bear.

I hope this sheds light on sex and consummation. Blessed are those who come together and fulfill the plans of Spirit. Whether together or apart they end. Amen.

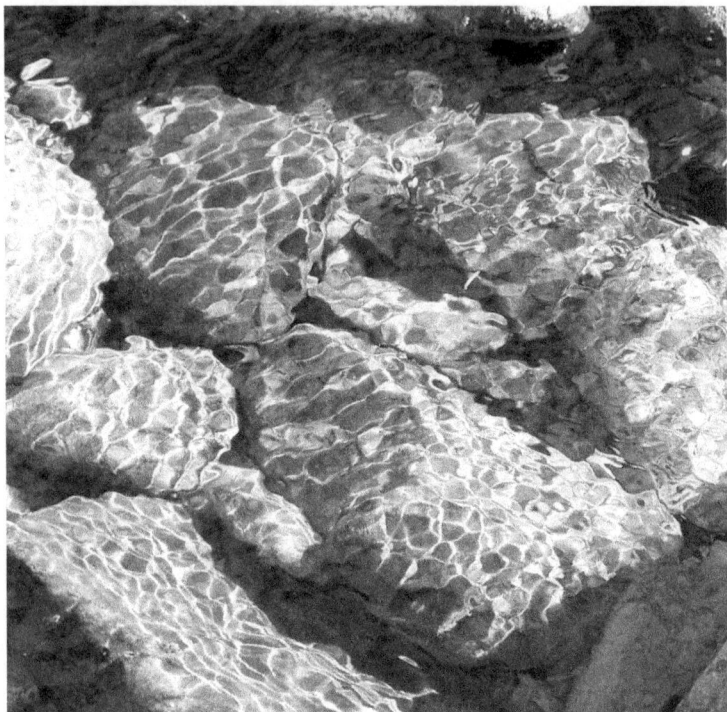

"The golden moments in the stream of life
rush past us, and we see nothing but sand;
the angels come to visit us and we only
know them when they are gone."

—GEORGE ELIOT

Jesus

I Have Awakened the Seed of Life Within You

Author's Observation: At first I saw Him radiant in peace, full of love, and ready to commit. I beckoned Him to speak to me, to teach me today.

Jesus held out His hands and urged me to come palm to palm, sacred heart to sacred heart, worthy mind to the greatest mind. The love and adoration I felt was overwhelming, and I shared my love for Him. Never has there ever been perfection, peace, and love that I have ever known in any Angel, man, woman, or Spirit body. As we connected within my heart, a seed began to grow. It grew threw my legs, down through my feet, and the roots went into the Earth... In my arms, out through my hands as branches to support and shelter others with. Up my torso, through my head, and above me it grew. Then he spoke:

I have awakened the seed of life within you. It will grow into the mighty tree of life. This I wish to do for all who would accept and connect with me. Today we will speak of the meaning of this. The seed represents the purpose you carry with you. You leave Heaven with only one.

This one seed/purpose lies within your care. It is up to you to use all of the things God has given you to help it grow. The seed sits within you, freely, wanting only to be used. Day

121

after day, your bodies glance at it and wonder of its purpose and what it will yield. Many of you wonder where to plant it and how to care for it. The seed should be planted within the Earth Mother within you. Every one of you has this part. It is the Earth from where your physical body was created. It is vast and large, waiting for the seed to be dropped in.

For some, it seems as a large dark space, and you not trusting to drop it in for fear of its diminishment. This is where your faith lies. If you trust enough to place this seed, then you must tend to it. The water that pours over it to thirst no more is the emotional part of you. But if your emotions are not as they should be, then it will be hard for them to water the seed that lies within.

Now, the mind is the sky. If it is clear, it will filter the light rays in to allow them to help the seed to grow. If the mind is not clear, then it blocks the rays and the seed never sprouts, or it ceases to continue growing. The light of course is your Spirit. That is the Spirit of God. It shines through day and night. It is always there. If you cannot see it, it is because your mind has become clouded with doubt, apprehension, fear, or worry. Do you know what it takes to clear the clouds? Stillness. When the wind ceases to blow in your mind, the clouds disappear. Still yourself every day so that these clouds do not hang over you and steal the light that so wants to nourish the seed within you.

Do you see? All of these things about you and within you reflect the Earth and its purpose. You are one and the same. Now let's talk about what happens when the tree has grown. It gives a home to all, shade, protection, food, and peace. When your purpose grows as it should, it will do all of these things. It will continue and grow to massive sizes.

Did you know that those who are fulfilling their spiritual purpose love trees? They have many trees around them. This is because it is a reflection of the same. In time, the tree within you will begin to decline. It will wither and die. It has served its purpose as have you, and ascension is soon to take place. But never fear because this tree sometimes leaves its seeds for others to carry on, plant, grow, and serve.

Today, I would ask you, have you planted your seed within the vast space of faith within you? Is your mind so clear that the full rays of the light of Spirit come down and nourish the seed to grow? Are you yielding fruit to all those around you? Are you giving shelter and shade to those who are tired and weak? Are you a home to the animals that need rest and a place to stay? This, my loves, is the seed of purpose. You possess this great seed. It is worth more than any gold coin. It is blessed and sacred. Holy and right. It is up to you to tend it. When you have done all of these things, the ascension is greater than anything can compare. Heaven's Gates are open wide, and all of Heaven and Earth is able to see the yield your seed gave.

Great is your reward for you have carried out a great plan—one that started before you arrived on the Earth. Many of you will call my name, and I will always come, but only some of you will feel me, receive me, and know me. Some of you cannot get past this physical realm. Know this . . . I change not. I will always come, and I will always love you. These are my words, and I am here to teach, remind, spark, and connect. I am like a world without end. I continue. I continue as I am, not as you would make me be, but as God himself/herself would make me be. I am a servant to the Lord, fulfilling the purpose or seed within me to better help you on your journey. I will always be. Amen.

> "Every blade of grass has an angel that bends over it
> and whispers, "Grow! Grow! . . . "
> —TALMUD

Seraphim

Don't Eat the Wrapper;
Choose the Candy

How many of you today are lonely and afraid? Did you know that these feelings are not real? They are like the wrapper on a piece of candy. What you want is the actual piece of candy, which is love. True, pure love is always sweet, always enough, always made just right. Why do you sit with the wrapper of candy and worry in fear and choose it over the candy? This does not make a lot of sense, does it? Did you know that you can have as much candy as you want, and you will never get sick? But the one condition is that you will always have to remove the wrapper of worry and fear. Take it off, and throw it away. You don't need it anymore to protect the love, the candy that is there. For some, this is too easy and too good to be true. Why would a loving God limit the amount of love? It is not God but you who limit it. You judge love as candy and think of it as just a treat here and there. In reality, love should be considered all of your food and all of your drink. Did you know that God never takes love away? God just sends more and more. You are the only one who tells God what is enough and what is not. Did you know that a child flourishes when it is loved? A plant grows more when it is told that it is loved.

An animal loses its fear when it is shown and feels love. Do not hesitate to spread it around. True, pure love never hurts anyone. It is gentle, kind, unconditional, and pure. Love one another, I tell you, and watch the world bloom into a full array of color, sound, and light. If you truly love, then you have nothing to lose.

Now, on another note, if you spread fear, you stop the flow. Life shrivels up, and animals, people, and plants will shrink away from you. Go sit outside, and let's see how much love you are allowing. See how the Earth, animals, and people come and go from you. This is a great experiment that will help you see where you are and what you are allowing. Do not hesitate to try this. Blessed is the Lord. For goodness, mercy, faith, and love remain forever and ever. Amen.

Angel Ishmael

Is Your Cup Half-Empty or Half-Full?

Today, we are going to talk about lust. First, what is it you deem lust and why do you prohibit it? It is simply the physical desire to copulate, nothing more. Lust is seeing a person only biologically, as nothing more. Lust only wants to merge with the physical, nothing more. Now, it is appropriate you should lust with the one you have committed to on all other levels. Lust or desire is good when you also have a mental, emotional, soul, and spiritual connection. Why? Because you are completely aligned:

- Spiritual—completing God's task, unconditional love, Spirit in form

- Soul—passion, heat, love, desire, comfort, deep connection

- Emotional—heartfelt, love, and beauty

- Mental—stimulation, connection with ideas, partnership

- Physical—lust, instinctual desire

Now, the reason why it is said to not covet another person's spouse or to lust is simply because that is all you will seem to have. The first level, nothing more. You see, this will cause you to feel more empty than full. Of course you may choose to have this temptation, you may have to feel this pulse race in your body, but you do not have to choose just this level. It will always leave you wanting more. Even though the desire was great and the physical union was wonderful, afterward you will feel the void of the other levels. It is because all of the other "glasses" or "cups" were not filled. Picture yourself as a level of shelves with glasses to be filled up. Your spiritual, soul, and mental glasses are contained in the head.

Your emotional glass is within your heart, and your physical glass is within your pelvic region. Now, you expect your partner to pour his/her essence into these cups and fill them up so that you need not feel empty. If your partner does not or you do not allow them to (because you are disconnecting), then afterward, you will know what remains empty. The cups lie within you. The only cup that never needs to be filled and that can fill up your other cups is the spiritual cup. It always remains full. It is never lacking, always ready to fill you. So many of you, when you look within to your cups, never get to the true spiritual cup. You only go to the soul cup level. It is because you think that is where God lives and is pure. You are mistaken.

Go up a level, and there you will find pureness and no

lack of any kind. Do you know that this is the everlasting life-giving waters Jesus spoke of? Spirit will pour itself into all of your cups and keep you full if you allow it. This is why priests, monks, and nuns may live secluded and celibate. They need no one to fill them but God.

This is the highest level of attainment, but it is not so easily researched. In your relationships, you are always pouring forth from one to another. If one of you does not pour enough or quick enough, the other gets hurt or offended. First, you must learn to fill yourself. Then, if another should offer you some of their life-giving water, then it will be only pleasure and peace. And yes, the two of these things can exist on the same plane, but only this way.

If you were to choose a life of emptiness of others and the joys of Spirit would you? Would you fill yourself first and then couple later? Doesn't it make more sense to become filled from a Source that has no end, rather than from a Source that does?

Become attached to the one true Source, the Source that has no end so that you will never find yourself wanting. You are instructed to love your God with all your heart, soul, and mind. You see these are levels. If you center these levels on attaching only to Source, there can never be emptiness. In Mark 10:21, Jesus says, "Take up the cross and follow me." This means to do the work of God, the work you agreed to do. And, in order to do this, you must consciously be connected to Spirit.

You see, the one thing that can affect, connect, tie, heal, and balance is at the center of the cross, the center of the cross and yourself. It is God/Spirit. When people suggest that you go within, they mean for you to travel from one of these levels to your God-center. There is always balance, harmony, joy, and peace there. If you tried to go without, then you will, at some point, feel a void. The only things that lie in the void are lack, fear, destitution, anger, pain, remorse, guilt, etc. You must turn within yourself. Now, if you connect with another, you will feel full at times as long as you keep the connections. It takes work to keep a connection with another.

Very seldom do two people overlap their crosses or completely connect each body to each body. This is a most powerful state and usually done by people who are "twin flames." A twin flame is the other half of you that is completely in line with who you are in this body and you in turn with them. Most Spirits only choose this if the soul does not need to be alone on any level in their incarnated life. With a twin flame, there is so much convergence that it is hard to tell where one begins and ends. When they are physically apart, their essence still surrounds the other. This is usually easy until one dies and passes on without the other, and then their challenge is to learn to go within and connect with God's Source to where their twin flame has fled. If they cannot accomplish this, then their pain is beyond their comprehension. As I said, this choice or connection does not happen often. Are you in understanding of this? May goodness and mercy bless you all of your days. May God keep you in His/Her Graces. Amen.

> *"To err is human: to forgive, divine,*
> *For fools rush in where angels fear to tread."*
>
> —ALEXANDER POPE

Saint Francis
and the Angels of Peace

Turn on the Light Switch
Within You

Many of you have often tried the path of poverty and feel as though you have failed. Today, I want to explain to you what the vow of poverty really means and why so many souls throughout the centuries have walked this path. Some of you have felt like in life that you were to give something up. Something of great value to you as a sacrifice or offering of love to God. In doing this, you humble yourself and open up your heart to the magic of divine will. Divine will can take you to places that you would otherwise have never experienced before. You become "wise as serpents and harmless as doves," as stated in Matthew10:16. When you offer to God something that is so important to you, God gives you something back that is beyond all value/peace.

True peace comes not from relying on yourself and providing for yourself, but by allowing all of this to come from

God. This walk is not always an easy one. Many people think they will starve and not have what they should, but this is only your body and flesh telling you that God and your Spirit is not enough to sustain you. Pray harder! The vow of poverty is taken by those who want to completely surrender everything to God. It is one of the most extreme vows to be taken. Many will suffer as they take this vow because they do not have the faith that they need, but we all have to start somewhere.

Now, you do not have to take a full vow of poverty, but you should offer up something of value to God, that will free you from your bondage and give you peace within. This could be putting out an entire garden and taking all of what you grow, your time, labor, and love with the crop and giving all of this to the poor. Do you see, you have given up something of great value and it will become an altar at which you surrender yourself and your works to God above? You are never more far from the light than what you are inside your house. In other words you can always turn on the light switch within you and begin to illuminate the world from the inside out. Thanks be to God. Amen.

"Think, in mounting higher, the angels would press on us, and aspire to drop some golden orb of perfect song into our deep, dear silence."

—ELIZABETH BARRETT BROWNING, *SONNET XXII*

Angel Muriel

Get Out of Your Box

Two things that are of importance today: the inside of the box and the outside of the box with regard to where are you standing and how you view both sides. The inside of the box represents the inside of you—all of the thoughts, emotions, fears, and work that is within you. Are you seeing and viewing all of these goings on or do you rather see the things around you? Is your perspective quiet but still contained? The inside holds you within and can be a very safe place to rest. It provides quiet in times of trouble and heartache. Today, I challenge you to walk out of the box, out of the security that you know to be true, and walk around in freedom. Open your container and let yourself out to be free to explore, look around you to see what boxes others have built. Most of the time, their house will embody the box they have put themselves in, for this life. It is very significant. Many of you are too afraid to step out of your own backyard and see how the world revolves and works. God created with you all of the universe for you to know. Not for you to sit and stay walled up within.

Many of you who cannot travel can always meditate and "travel" in that sense, but that would ask you to leave your box. See the walls you have built each brick and why. What are the reasons for them? Each time you mortar in a brick, walling yourself and shutting down, you are really cutting yourself off and seeing yourself as separate, which you are not. Here is an example: a splinter or foreign object comes into the body. The foreign object represents fear, anger, hate, envy, etc. Now you cocoon that foreign object and create a cyst to contain it. Well, sometimes in life you do the same thing by walling yourself in from the rest of the "body" and focusing the attention on the negative.

How many of you have spent your life looking at your cocooned anger and refusing to let the "body" and others outside the "body" (Spirit, Angels; they are the doctors and nurses) help you excise this and let it go. Why are you cocooning and damming up? It is because anger gives you something. You have to figure out what that something is. Is it an identity, authority, control, pity? What is it? Now, on another note, the Tree of Life grows within you. The tree is the energetic structure of the spirit energy that emanates from the highest dimensions and into the third dimension. It is deep inside of you, and that means you have the power to heal yourself. You harbor it like you would a ship or boat, but how often do you use it? Use the power that you have within your true self. You are never disconnected from the Creator. Amen.

"*Every breath of air and ray of light and heat,
every beautiful prospect, is, as it were, the skirts
of the (angel's) garments, the waving robes
of those whose faces see God.*"

—JOHN HENRY NEWMAN

Seraphim

Are You a Maple or an Evergreen?

Author's Observation: Glorious sapphire blue radiates all around him. He is joined by two others of the same rank. He knows no sorrow, only the pure delight of God. There is no judgment only that of knowing. They are here; they surround the space above me. They stand and wait, ready to speak the language they were created to speak. But my soul began to speak, "I am my Creator's and my Creator is mine. I will dwell in the holiness of my creation, and I will bring the truth from my inner core. I shall always proclaim the true light that is within me, and I will forever rest in the glory of the one who made me. I am my creator's, and my creator is mine. Within the highest planes to the lowest valleys, I will be accompanied always by the Angels God has created for me and mine. I will forever serve my Creator in fulfilling my purpose. By this, my placement has been for use, and I exist into the next realm. Woe to those who have helped me on my journey by bending my knees and also by helping me stand. I have become what Creator wants of me, and by doing this, I will return to exist in the realm of peace."

Other Angels begin to file in all around me. Slowly they step toward me. Colors are all different yet radiant and pure. They envelop me and ask of me to open my heart to this other realm. This realm only knows love. It lacks for nothing; it is always complete in form. Angels speak:

Today, we wish to talk about the trees. Just as there are different types of trees, there are different types of people, just as there are different purposes. For example, there are fruit, blossom, nut, berry, and evergreen trees.

The first lesson is to accept the differences in the trees and their purposes, because your Lord God made them all. The next step would be to honor these trees and purposes because your Lord God had a reason for each yield. Now let's talk about the yield. What are you yielding? Is it fruit, which is nourishment for people and animals? Is it berries, which are nourishment for people and animals? Is it nut, which is nourishment for people and animals? Is it blossoms, which have beauty and sweet nectar? Or is it staying evergreen: always remaining constant in your giving? Do you give for a season or for all year? When you begin to honor all of the trees (people) God has made and their yield (purposes), then you will begin to understand that you are just a tiny bit in the large creation of God.

You see, you have a purpose, but so do the rest. The most important step is recognizing. If you do not recognize, then you never fully begin your path—fully aware, fully open, fully ready. Do not be afraid for where God has placed you on the Earth is exactly where you are to be, even as uncomfortable as it may seem. Some of you feel like you are a pine in the middle of a bunch of maples. The key is not to think you are wrong or they are wrong because that would be saying that God makes mistakes, and God does not make mistakes! The highest attainment would be acceptance of them and yourself.

Honor their "mapleness," and you will be your "pine self." There is no shame in who you truly are and who you have chosen to be on this Earth. For example, a Korean child is adopted by a white English family and is raised among them. His yield is being an Eastern herbalist while his family's yield is in traditional Western medicine. That is his yield, his calling, and if he did something else other than this, he would not be yielding what he was made for. He knows and you know exactly what is within you. You just have to let it produce itself and not hold it back. You have to trust when you first begin to bud that it is as it should be. You are not "weird" or "different" because in God's world, we all are as we should be. The more you begin to trust the budding, then the blooming, then the yielding, the more you will begin to breathe!

The breath is the breath of living energy that gives you the courage and knowledge of your purposes. You have been picked, chosen, and ordained, each and every one of you, on this planet. You have the right to know your yield; ask of it. You have the right to the sun, water, and air. Ask for it for your growth and purpose, and when you have finished, your body that held you will decline and fall back to the Earth to continue to give. Thanks be to God. Amen.

*"Reputation is what men and women think of us.
Character is what God and the angels know of us."*
—THOMAS PAINE

Angel Samuel

---

*Everything Turns
Back to God*

All is not lost when you decide to turn your "car" into another direction. So many people believe that they make a mistake when they choose to go a different path, or take another road. It is just simply that all of the roads are all connected, and they ALL lead to God. Many think that where they have gone before is in vain or that they are betraying another. It is simply that they have turned onto a different path, and the people around them will either stay or go. A person's judgment of choice is not based on who stays or who goes but on what level of place the person has within. Sometimes it is meant for you to travel a road that seems deserted and you feel alone, but when you travel this road hopefully you will begin to see us Angels, and God, and appreciate the beauty God created on the road because there is none there to distract you from it.

Everyone needs quiet time. Everyone needs reflection time. So then why do you think just because you have few humans around you that this is bad? That you have made a wrong turn? Did you never stop to think that there is always a plan? So then why do you think you are ever off course? Because other men tell you are? Don't ask men; ask your Heavenly Father and Mother. Yes, I said Mother. Why is it you should believe that God has only male attributes? Isn't that like saying there is a great tree, but there are never any leaves that grow on it? You see God is both; God is all! God is the way, God is the truth, and God is life. So then, if this be the case, why do you think you can separate yourself from God? It is only your focus. It would be like a child covering his eyes and saying that no one can see him. He is "making believe." He thinks this is the truth, but it is not. Just like when you say, "There is no God," or "God wasn't there when I was molested," or "I will go to Hell, and God will no longer see me." Do you really think any of this is true? Well, it is not. You simply have your eyes shut. You are "making believe."

There are moments in your life you say you are alone, but that is only your mind's perception, which happens to always be false. You say you are lonely, and that is a false pride of your heart. You say that you are angry, and that is because your soul fears. All of these are illusions not to be trusted or to put much weight on. It would be like looking into water and seeing these things being reflected, and while they appear almost real, when you reach out to them or step into them, the water parts and nothing is there. Do not base who you are by reflecting these untruths into the water. That is not the real you. Close your eyes to who you are and look within yourself. That will reveal a great light that shines for all the world. Others will wonder where you found your light, and when they ask, you can tell and show them they are light also.

Be not afraid of anything, because everything turns back to God! There is a special time for everything and a purpose under the Heavens. Do not wonder who you are. Wake up and know. You are a child of God—a fragment, a light, a reflection of God. All you have to do is shine. In Ephesians 5:8, it says, "For you were once darkness, now you are the light in the Lord. Walk as children of light." In Matthew 5:14–16, it says, "You are the light of the world. A city that is set on a hill cannot be hidden. Nor do they light a lamp and put it under a basket, but on a lamp stand, and it gives light to all that are in the house. Let your light so shine before men, that they may see your good works and glorify your Father in Heaven." In John 1:4–5, it says, "In Him was life, and the life was the light of men. And the light shines in the darkness, and the darkness did not comprehend it." In Psalms 27:1, it says, "The Lord is my light and my salvation; whom shall I fear? The Lord is the strength of my life; of whom shall I be afraid?" Thanks be to God. Amen.

Mary Magdalene

---

*The Truth Will Always
Find You*

Hello, so we meet again—this world and me. There are many things I would like to say and teach, but there is just one today that is the most important. I am here today to reveal the most intimate and most often asked question, "Was I the lover and spouse of Jesus Christ?" My answer would be yes and no. Yes, we had close relations. We were wed not in the Temple but outside of Temple rule. We were not formerly recognized because of my background. I was not a prostitute, but I was not a virgin.

I had unwed relations with a man who was much older than me. My life had seemed a scandal and in shambles when Jesus met me. He showed me how to forgive myself and stop judging myself for the virginity that I had lost. It was then that I began to fall in love with him, not only as a human but as a spiritual teacher. These talks and teachings went on for several years, and at one point, I drew closer to him than all others. This was a hard and difficult thing for the others to accept. They hated that I understood on the deeper levels. Jesus confided in me things that he did not confide in others. In order to complete the balance, I grew in knowledge and love and soon the Savior took me as an equal into a sacred partnership. As we entered into the holiness of the merging of both male and female, we were completing God's plan for us and all others. And after this, there was no more. I left and moved after the crucifixion to create another part of my life. I had no more spouses or children, but I tried to teach others what Christ had taught me.

Some of these teaching are written down. These are sacred documents stored away in a great Temple in Egypt. For the most part, other nations would not accept my teachings because they had a certain place for women, and I broke out of that place. The Egyptians far better understood the similarities of both male and female and saw us as equally important. Now, in your children's lifetime, these holy writings will be discovered, and it will change what we, as a human race, knows now. You see, God will always bring the truth to you, but it is up to you if you accept it or not. This is what Jesus meant when he said, "The truth will always find you." That was no threat, just a fact. If men are unable to accept truth, then they will kill it, suppress it, hide it, and bury it. But I tell you this, it will arise over and over again until it is accepted by all. Live your life today not by the untruths, but by the truths. Then you will be set free. Amen.

Angel Ezechiah

You Cannot Destroy What God Is

Author's Observation: Angels of all colors and properties come to me and speak comfort but also truth. Today, they want to teach about many wives, many mansions, and many lives.

What do you believe the order of marriage is? We have waited to speak to you for some time on this subject. I will tell you, the order of marriage is a binding earthly contract that says I agree to manifest, learn lessons, and love unconditionally with you. How does one know the length of a marriage? When these options no longer seem to be what one or both need anymore, there is a separation and a moving onward. Is this a sin? No, it is a decision. There is a difference. A sin is something that occurs or is created and is not the very highest vibration. For example, adultery is not the highest vibration because of deception and untruth. This causes pain. But what if there is no deception or untruth? What if all parties are in agreement? This is a decision. Then how can it be a sin? Why is it that men choose to say what God's rules are and are not?

Did God create love? Is God unconditional love? Aren't you to be as God? Then why, if there is complete truth would loving more than one soul be sinful or incorrect? It is only because man thought it is better with one and easier to have only one wife instead of many. Also, whenever there is more than two, the unit has to learn constantly to balance the shifting energy of three or more. It is more difficult to make major decisions in life with more than two. There is a greater risk of emotional and mental pain. This is why man thought that surely God would not want their pain, and so it became easier with two instead of three or more. Are you understanding? These were man's decisions, not God's. God has several real truths, but we refuse to call them rules because rules can be broken. God's truths can never be broken.

You cannot destroy what God is: unconditional love, peace, and all that will exist forever. When you are not at peace, then you are not seeing God, and you forget unconditional love. Hook back into the truth. To finish this analogy or lesson today is of vital importance to the author and all who will read this. The heart can never be truly broken. This is an illusion of separateness. Do you understand? An illusion.

Hearts were not made to break; they were made to feel, and they can feel anyway they choose. The heart is not so much a physical dimension but an ethereal dimension. This means it is eternal. What do you want your heart to feel eternally? Love, laughter, and joy or pain, sorrow, and fear? Why not choose the things that are real?

Now addressing marriage: you will see as all of you heighten your awareness of what is truly real, that marriage is simply a union—usually two coming together as one. But why not three or four? Why is it you say only two can become one? That is simply your perception. It is like a pie. Most of you cut your pie in half, and these are the two souls coming together to make the whole. Why not three or four? Don't you see that you are still all in the same pie? In other words, you are still connected, still a part of God and still merging.

Why is it that you have this false ego of conquer and be conquered? Don't you see you are everything and everything is you? There is really no conquering. Again, an illusion. Find your way, find your light, and find the spark that guides you through. Not just when things are dark, but also when things are light. You will know that it is truth when you finally reach peace. You can never separate from the light, just like you can never separate from each other. Know thyself. When you do, you will recognize one another. Then you will see that you all are truly married. Think about this. I leave you with this: Can light ever truly be separated, and if it can, does it change? You don't stop living because someone doesn't accept the way you breathe. Amen.

*"Angels are speaking to all of us . . .
some of us are only listening better."*
—ANONYMOUS

Angels Malachi and Auriana

Stop Fighting Where Life Is Taking You

Changes: They are all around you, but you still seem to be shocked when they occur. Why? Why is it that when we tell you to let go and flow with life and the changes, you fail to flow but feel as if you will drown in the water. Stop fighting where life is taking you. The I-Ching quotes, "It is only change that is at work here." Do you not trust God? Has God not proved Himself/Herself to you over and over again? It is all under God's domain—there is nothing that is not. When your child or a child is in trouble or drowning, would you not rescue them? How much more then would God do for you? Do you feel you are not worthy? Why is that? Why do you think you do not deserve God's saving, healing, loving ability? Is it that you do not want it? Can you not accept God's love? Maybe it is because you do not know who you are. You are worthy, you are God's child, and you always deserve help. We are here to help you now. What is it that you want to know?

The question is: Why do situations go bad?

Why do you deem it bad? Maybe this is for the highest good. Doesn't everything flow in the highest good if you create it that way? The situation was created so that both parties could see that things, people, and aspirations are not always as they began. You have learned that rules change when people's intentions and emotions change. How is it that people promise, yet change a month later? It is because they and you are growing—growing in the direction you are to go in.

Nothing stays the same. This can make people feel depressed because they feel helpless and as if they have been stripped of their power. They can feel naked, vulnerable, judged, abandoned, and sickened. Did you know that is how they are to feel? You were supposed to feel this in order to surrender—surrender to the highest good for you and for all. It is said—and it is true—by Mansur al-Hallaj that "When God takes a heart, he empties it of all that is not Him." This is what we mean by surrender. When you surrender, you lose who you think you are to become the truth of what God knows you are. This is called the great awakening. Everyone seeks to have this revelation and can find it in very different ways, but even if you do not seek it, life will give it to you anyway. There is something very beautiful about surrender, and it is this: when you surrender to the highest good, the highest good is all that there is.

There are no worries, and there is only a letting go. Peace soon follows and the pathway becomes clear. Not by your light will you see clearly but by Gods light with yours. In learning to surrender, you gain true life. By giving up everything that people told you that you were, and you thought you might be, you allow the truth of your existence to permeate through your physical body and consciousness. Have faith that everyone that walks a path will be brought to the Gateway of Surrender. And it will be your decision to bend your knees and let go or to stand at the Gateway and never experience the spiritual path that lies ahead. Ram Dass says, "The spiritual journey is individual, highly personal. It cannot be organized or regulated. It isn't true that everybody should follow one path. Listen to your own truth."

Woe to those who do not bend, for peace will elude them, and they will cry out to God and ask, "Why have you forsaken me?" God's reply will simply be "I have not forsaken you but you have brought your growth to a halt. I sit beside you and wait for the surrender of who you think you are so that I can show you what is real."

Find peace in the words that you have read, the words that have been spoken to you. "For God so loved the world that he gave his only begotten son." This means that the world is the ego and the false consciousness, and the son is you, Spirit. These are working together to bring all of the creation back to the light from where it began. Peace be with you. Amen.

"It was pride that changes angels into devils;
it is humility that makes men as angels."

—SAINT AUGUSTINE

Saint John and Angel Angelica

Light or Dark? You Choose

Today, we want to talk to you about Lucifer and his dominion. They take form only in your mind. In truth, they are low or dark energy that runs rampant, looking for a place to rest. They can only come in and rest if you invite them. How do you invite them? By forgetting to love. You see, your physical body and your soul always have a choice. This is also known as free will. Free will was given to the soul to help it choose a path to learn all the lessons it needed to learn. On either side of the path is light and dark. You can choose to walk close to the Spirit, light, or you can choose to walk close to the darkness. Either way you choose, you will learn. Throughout your lifetimes, you weave a path back and forth.

Many who understand this concept begin to understand what humans call balance: Walking the middle between both energies, seeing that each is necessary for soul growth. If everyone chose the light at every second, then you would no longer be in the physical body. You would simply ascend! Now, we want you to think why a soul would consciously choose the dark. It is because they have forgotten their origin, where they were made and what they were made from. Darkness tells them they are anything other than worthy and loving, and somehow they begin to believe it. Do you want to know why? It is called guilt. They do not know how or haven't taken the spiritual time to forgive. Forgiveness is a whole other topic that we will be discussing in the last part of this book.

Guilt is the one thing, the one emotion, that traps you and chains you to believe the darkness is what you deserve. With the new information that has been given to the world on manifestation and karma, one should begin to understand that God does not condemn the soul, nor does God judge the soul.

For instance, you are the student willing to take the class, take a test, then check your own answers. If they are not sufficient, then you will simply choose to take the class and the test again. God is the instructor but never the punisher. So then, if all you have to do is take the test over, why should you feel guilty for not doing as well the first time around? It doesn't make much sense. Then why do you punish yourselves? Punishment was invented by the ego to control; the light did not invent it. The light is God; the light is pure love. Let me ask you this: if you had a child who is being mean to another child, what would you do? Your ego would tell you to punish the child and show him/her right and wrong, but your Spirit would say to hold both children and pour your love into them until all fear and abuse vanished. Have you ever thought that when people are mean, cruel, angry, and violent, they simply need tremendous amounts of love and counseling? You would simply change their improper thoughts by shifting their vibration to love.

Many parents are now counseling their children and putting them in timeouts, but not holding them and loving them until their vibration changes. When it changes, you will know.

They will not resist you; they will relax, become receptive, and remember what they have done. They simply need to remember they are love, and love is all there is! Everything else is false. That is why anything else other than love feels bad, because your truth should always be love.

Now, why does the darkness exist? Because you keep creating it. Yes, you. The soul you. When there is a demonic possession present, whom do you call on for help? God, love. If there is sickness, whom do you call on? God, love. Get the point? When you have forgotten who you are, darkness will come in and push you to the light. When everyone remembers who they are, darkness will no longer be needed by, or created by, your soul. You will finally accept that love is real, and that is all there is . . . LOVE. Praise be to God the Father and Mother for the truth that sets us free from the burdens of sin and forgetting.

Here is a Universal Prayer: "God, you are the Source of all that is, and I am your worthy child. Give unto me what should be granted to me, and keep me all the days of my life. For you are merciful, loving, generous, and kind. You are my eternal creator, and I am yours forever." Amen.

If I speak in the tongues of men and of angels,
    but have not love,
I am only a resounding gong or a clanging cymbal.
If I have the gift of prophecy and can fathom all
    mysteries and all knowledge,
and if I have a faith that can move mountains,
    but have not love, I am nothing.
If I give all I possess to the poor and surrender
    my body to the flames,
but have not love, I gain nothing.

Love is patient, love is kind. It does not envy,
    it does not boast, it is not proud.
It is not rude, it is not self-seeking, it is not
    easily angered, it keeps no record of wrongs.
Love does not delight in evil but rejoices with
    the truth.
It always protects, always trusts, always perseveres.
Love never fails. But where there are prophecies,
    they will cease;
where there are tongues, they will be stilled;
    where there is knowledge, it will pass away.
And now these things remain: faith, hope and love.
    But the greatest of these is love.

—BIBLE, 1 CORINTHIANS 13:1–8, 13

> *"Man was so created by the Lord as to be able while living in the body to speak with spirits and angels, as in fact was done in the most ancient times; for, being a spirit clothed in a body, he is one with them."*
>
> —EMANUEL SWEDENBORG

Angel Ishmael and Female Seraphim

Forgiveness Silences the Ego and Changes Dark into Light

Author's Observation: It has been obvious to me that the last part of this book should be focused on forgiveness. Without forgiveness, we lose the ability to go forward on our soul path, and without forgiveness, we seem to always be tied to the dock, our boats never moving forward as they should. I for one choose to sail the waters and see all things and have all the experiences that one should have on the ocean of life.

Webster's Dictionary says that forgiveness means to pardon, or to give up resentment of, or to cease to feel resentment against. How many times are we asked every day to forgive, to untie the rope that binds us to the dock and sail free, and how many times do we forgive? Who is the one who asks us to forgive? God, the light within us, our true selves? Or maybe the God that is in the other person. Does it really matter from which Source forgiveness is asked? I believe Jesus instructed the disciples to forgive their brother not just seven times, but seventy times seven. There can be no true peace without the forgiveness of this illusion that we call the reality of this world. I ask all of my brothers and sisters who are reading this book to remember what James said in James 4:14: "For what is your life? It is even a vapor that appears for a little time, and then vanishes away."

We are simply passing through, and this is not our true home. Do not hold on to the things of this world, because you are not of this world. Your home resides somewhere else, and by forgiving the very core of you, the very essence of you will be reminded of where your true home lies. When we forgive, we are saying that we understand that nothing of this world is perfect and that it is just a school to learn. We are all down here learning, but learning what? We are learning how to get back home—to remerge with the light that made us and, for once and for all, to put the ego to rest.

Forgiveness silences the ego and changes dark into light. It destroys fear, and it lets us out of our prison. Not only do I ask you to forgive one another, but I would ask you to forgive yourselves. James 2:13 says, "For judgment is without mercy to the one that has shown no mercy. Mercy triumphs over judgment."

I am asking you today to give yourselves mercy, because until you give it to yourself, it is very difficult to *show mercy to your brothers and sisters. Christ said, "What you do to the least, you do to the whole." What this means is we are formed as one body in God, and so if you show no mercy to one person, the whole body feels it. This is why Christ said, "What is hidden in the dark will be brought into the light." This was not a threat; it was a fact. I will pray for all of you daily, and I ask for your prayers also. Together, we can untie our boats and sail the waters that we came to sail, and I hope as we pass by one another, that we recognize one another's souls and lend a helping hand. May God Bless you, and keep you all the days of your lifetime.*

In Matthew 5:43–48, it says, "You have heard that it was said. 'You shall love your neighbor and hate your enemy.' Jesus said 'But I say to you, love your enemies, bless those who curse you, do good to those who hate you, and pray for those who spitefully use you and persecute you, that you may be sons with your Father in Heaven; for He makes his sun rise on the evil and on the good, and send rain on the just and on the unjust. For if you love those who love you, what rewards have you? Do not even the tax collectors do the same? And if you greet your brethren only, what do you do more than others? Do not even the tax collectors do so? Therefore you shall be perfect, just as your Father in Heaven is perfect.'"

In John 13:34–35, it says, "A new commandment I give to you, that you love one another; as I have loved you, that you also love one another. By this all will know that you are my disciples, if you have love for one another." Then, in John 15:12–13, it says, "This is my commandment, that you love one another as I have loved you. Greater love has none than this, than to lay down one's life for his friends."

What does *life* mean in this particular commandment? Be
Jesus. Life means your thoughts of this reality based on your
judgment of the world. In other words, you are to lay down
your judgment of others and love them. When judgment is
lost, fear no longer exists, and you can only see what truly is.
For example, if a child were to go out and play in the mud, as
the mother, would you simply wash the child off after he has
had his romp or would you judge and condemn him for getting his clothes dirty?

Do you see that forgiveness and love wash the soul clean
of iniquity or sinfulness, or muddiness? Don't you think that
is much easier to hand your brother or sister a pale of water
and a bar of soap than wasting all of your time on negative
perception? But how would you know this if you had not first
washed yourself clean?

Christ commanded in Matthew 7:3–4, "And why do you
look at the speck in your brother's eye, but do not consider
the plank in your own eye? Or how can you say to your
brother, 'Let me remove the speck from your eye: and look, a
plank is in your own eye?' This is what John the Baptist and
Christ were doing whenever they were baptizing the ones who
would come to them for solace. It is not about washing the
physical body, but proclaiming, "I have had an experience that
has soiled my soul, and now I choose to wash myself clean."

No one sin or muddy experience is greater than the other.
Mud is mud, and it should have no more judgment other than
that. You are not of this world, so what you should be forgiving is your thoughts that you are of this world. You should be
forgiving the fact that you have forgotten where you come
from and begin to help yourself and others remember. John
the Baptist said, "I baptize you with water and repentance."

In other words, John was saying that *repentance*—in this context—means, *I understand that experience, have felt the mud, and I choose to take a shower and go forward without judgment.* John also said that Christ would baptize you with the Holy Spirit and Fire. In other words, Christ is to help you remember who you are and help you to find your soul purpose, or your fire that burns within. They both understood that judgment, or condemnation, is not necessary nor is it needed to get a clear picture of your life experience. Forgiveness is what is at work here, and you cannot have forgiveness without love and mercy. This is the Trinity, but in order to really be able to help your brothers and sisters wash the mud from themselves, you must first wash the mud from your own soul.

Experience, in this reality you call Earth, is everything. In order to understand something, you have to feel it many times. Mud simply clouds your view of your Heavenly reality. So, to see where you are going, you must first clean the mud from the windshield of your car. Do you understand? Are you understanding that you should have no judgment for the mud, nor the mud being on you or your brothers and sisters? It is simply part of the experience on Earth.

Here is another aspect of forgiveness: if you clean your soul or your windshield of the mud, and yet you still feel guilt in obtaining the mud, then what have you gained? Why is it that humans feel that even after they have taken the steps to clean themselves, they still feel guilty in experiencing the mud? It is because your mind wants you to feel fear constantly. It wants you to think that you are always on the edge of a cliff, about ready for the end to come. But I ask you, can mud on your face or from the top of your head to the feet kill you? No, because you are eternal, my friend.

Your brain wants you to believe that this life is all that matters, but I tell you that this life is a millisecond in your infinite existence, and a small amount of mud never hurt anybody. It is your choice. You can pull in and go through the carwash and get back on your soul path, or you can let the mud build up until you lose sight of your direction. What have you gained? Mud is mud, sin is sin, and there is no real reason to let it hinder you or give you negative emotions. Forgiveness means letting go. Forgiveness means that that particular experience no longer affects you. You have chosen love over everything else, and when you do this, you set yourself and everyone on the planet free from thinking that this life is all there is.

Do not seek the things that moth and dust corrupt as Christ instructed, but seek the things that are everlasting. You, my friend, are everlasting, and so is the Source of where you come from, and so are your brothers and sisters. When they are muddy and begin to sling mud on others, give them a bar of soap and a bucket of water and help them to wash themselves clean. In other words, give them love and help them forgive themselves. For there is no greater gift than that.

Forgiveness, love, and mercy—this is the Trinity. This is what we speak of; this is everlasting. Peace to all of you who have made it to the end of this book, and we know because we see that forgiveness is at work here in your lives. You picked up this book because you knew there were messages for your soul. Messages that would free your soul, wash it clean, and give it peace. We hope that just as we know constantly, that God is us, and dwells within us, that you will also know this too. We Angels are messengers and workers for the light. We knew that as humanity fell to this Earth and took on a form that there may be times when you would forget who you are and from where you came. We are the ones who are in charge of remembering. We know you from the beginning, and we have always existed with you, as we have all existed with God.

In Matthew 4:6, it says, "He shall give his Angels charge over you, in their hands they shall bear you up, lest you dash your foot against the stone." So we ask you to not jump out of our hands, nor to fight us as we are helping you get down your path. Do not resist our presence in your life, for we bring the will of God. There are many things to come that your human mind would tell you to be afraid of, but we tell you to forgive your human mind and have faith in your Source. Remember, you are neither of this world, nor will you rest here. You are simply passing through like the wind.

The Earth will continue to go through massive changes, and people will fear if they do not know from where they came. We tell you that we are workers of the light, and the darkness cannot stand in our presence. We tell you that our mission is to bring you back home and to help you wash the mud from your souls in the process. We tell you we have no judgment of the mud or you, because we see your eternal being. We tell you that we have unconditional love for you and that your birth out of the physical body and back into the Heavenly realms is but a celebration. We tell you that as soon as you come into your true conscious being, no longer do you have to reincarnate on the Earth to try to remember. We know your fears, we feel your sorrows, and we understand the depths of despair that your soul chooses to sink into, but we are here to pick you up, clean you off, and show you the way home.

There will never be a time that we are not with you, and there will never be a time when we cease to exist. As Adam and Eve fell into the Garden, we were created to bring them back home, and we have been trying for what seems like, in Earth years, centuries to get all of the Christ consciousness back together. We know and we see of a day when Earth will no longer be needed, and that room in the mansion will be sealed up and be used no more. We see a day where the Christ consciousness will be whole, and creation will start not because it forgot anything, but because it finally knows who it is and chooses to create in other dimensions. The Earth reality was created because of the forgetting, of one single forgetting, and so your world as you know it came into existence—your world of the knowledge of light and dark, or what you call good or evil.

We say mud and water. We say that in remembering, you leave the world of forgetting. This is your ticket home. Home to a place that you really belong, and home to a place where forgiveness is not needed because there is no judgment. Forgiveness is only needed in this world because you have had the thought you have done something wrong. This is why we bring to you, in the last part of this book, that forgiveness of what you think is here, mercy of yourself and others, and love for the whole planet will bring you back home. These are the steps to your freedom. Freedom of the physical body and the separated consciousness that thinks you do not deserve the light of God. Would it make any sense to you to have a big beautiful fire, and a spark from that fire jump away from its creator, and isolate itself feeling that it does not deserve to be part of the whole? Do you honestly think that a spark would have these thoughts? It does not. It burns in its true form, so why don't you?

We will tell you that as you try to come into your true consciousness, you will meet resistance often. People will tell you that you are wrong, and your brain will tell you that you should feel fearful or guilty, that you would try to remember your origin. Resistance will keep you in chains and keep you miserable. This is why Christ said, "If you gain the whole world but you lose your soul, you have gained nothing." It is not what other people think of you; it is what you know of yourself. Why do you think Christ and every disciple, and every martyr and saint who has ever lived, have met major resistance on their path of remembering?

This is simply part of the experience, and with faith and trust in God, and us at your side, you will push through the resistance and come into your true nature. Do not seek what the world seeks, but seek that which lies within yourself. Seek that which is beyond this world and is the place of origin. From where does a child come? The physical body is made from the physical, but from where do the life force, the breath, the Spirit, and the soul come? It comes from another place that you call home, and when your body is failing, your soul will remember that it has a home. Do not seek to follow another's life path, but seek your own life path. Follow no man, but follow the light that is within each man.

Forgive what was, forgive what is, and look beyond this world of illusion, only in doing this will you find your freedom in the Heavens. Hold your faith steady, for in faith there is no despair. In faith, you are anchored in your true creator, and none can remove your view of reality. Hold true to the

love that sits within your Spirit for that is the pure unconditional love of God. You always have this like a Band-Aid in
your medicine cabinet. When someone is hurting or when
you are hurting, it is always there to access to put over the
wound and heal. You feel pain because you think this world
is real. Do you honestly think Christ felt pain on the cross?
We tell you he felt very little, if any at all. Why is this? Because
he knew he was not of this world, and he was no longer connected to his physical body. Jesus said to the criminals,
"Assuredly I say to you, today you will be with me in Paradise.
And at the moment when Jesus did feel any pain, he cried out,
"Eloi, Eloi, lama sabachthani?" which means, "My God, my
God, why have you forsaken me?" And, at that moment,
darkness came upon the Earth, and the veil of the Temple was
torn in two.

The veil represents the wall between God and you. Christ
came in to tear down the wall so that you no longer have to
go to a priest but can go to God yourself. Christ was saying
that you no longer needed a priest, but you are the priest
yourself, and you can step into the Holy of Holies without
fear. And Jesus cried out, "Father, into your hands I commit
my spirit," and then he was released from the physical body.
Also, it is important to note that as Christ was in the Garden before his crucifixion, his heart was heavy and his mind
knew of what was to come. We, the Angels were his comfort
(Luke 22:43), "Then an Angel appeared to him from Heaven,
strengthening Him." Do you remember what Jesus' last prayer
for those around him was? As stated in Luke 23:34, "Father,
forgive them for they do not know what they do."

Do you see Christ knew and understood that forgiveness,
mercy, and love are the only ways home? All of you, who say

that you are true Christians, should remember these most important things about whom you refer to as your savior. For all of you who are not Christians, you should remember these teachings anyway, since you see Christ as a Master Teacher. We say he came, he taught, he loved, he forgave, and he ascended. What better example of freedom is there than that?

Forgiveness equals freedom, mercy equals peace, and love sends you Home. We pray that as you go through your daily life, you will remember and know that you have a Guardian Angel and many other Angels who accompany you. Even as the darkness enfolds you, we never leave you as we never left Christ or the criminals. You see, to us it does not matter how little or how much mud you have on you. We love you just the same. Open up your mind and heart to us, and we will speak to you and guide you. You all have the ability to see and hear; you just have to remember that you can. For those of you who need help for this, there will always be a teacher sent to you. For God loves you so much that He gives you everything you need to get back home. Matthew 6:25–34 states, "Therefore I say to you, do not worry about your life, what you will eat, or what you will drink; nor about your body, what you will put on. Is not life more than food and the body more than clothing? Look at the birds of the air, for they neither sow nor reap, nor gather into barns; yet your Heavenly Father feeds them. Are you not of more value than they? Which of you by worrying can add one cubit to his stature? So why do you worry about clothing? Consider the lilies of the field, how they grow: they neither toil nor spin; and yet I say to you that even Solomon in all his glory was not arrayed like one of these. Now if God so clothed the grass of the field, which today is, and tomorrow is thrown into the oven, will he not much more cloth you, oh you of little faith? Therefore do not worry, saying, 'What shall we eat?' or 'What shall we drink?' or 'What shall we wear?' for all of these things the Gentiles seek. For your Heavenly Father knows you need all these things. But seek first the Kingdom of God and His righteousness, and all these things shall be added to you. Therefore do not worry about tomorrow, for tomorrow will worry about its own things. Sufficient for the day is its own trouble." Peace be with you, peace we bring to you, and peace you will find on your journey home. Remember we are always with you. Amen.

"If there is anything that keeps the mind open
to angel visits, and repels the ministry to evil,
it is pure human love."

—N.P. WILLIS

Council of Angels
(Archangels Gabriel, Michael, Uriel, and Raphael)

Questions & Answers

Today, you have many questions. Events, situations, and even documentaries on Heaven and Hell have made you curious and inquisitive. So we will answer your questions directly.

Explain to me the meaning of "Everything is not as it seems to be."

We are referring to your perspectives and others' perspective on reality—how you and all of your colleagues have constructed *what is* and *what is not*. Do you not realize that all that is is God? Everything else exists only in this dimension. What we want people to understand is that problems, suffering, pain, and unrest exist only on Earth in several dimensions. What if, at the center of the Earth, is Hell? Just another dimension on the Earth. You see, the Earth's dimensions are layers, just as Heaven's dimensions are layers. Yes, there are layers, as the Bible refers to it as Jacob's "ladder" to Heaven. Ascension for most did not happen in a snap. It was a progression up the ladder or dimensions to Heaven.

Why do you think we Angels could move up and down?

We are not Spirits paired with souls, but rather the purest thoughts of God. That is how we can come and go. Now let's talk about when the Bible refers to not being able to cross from Heaven into Hell. The Spirits/souls that have begun to ascend up and out cannot go back. Jesus came and insured you with this. This is why he possessed the keys to death. Why do you think he rose again? He was ensuring you that you will not obtain ascension in one life, incarnate, "mess up," and descend to Hell, but through him, we will begin to ascend. This is called grace and forgiveness.

God edited your plan down here. You see, God saw that the original karmic laws—"An eye for an eye and a tooth for tooth"—were not working. Not many were making ascensions and continuing upward. So you needed one love, one sacrifice, or one savior to save you from these descensions. Now you are not cast into Hell by all of your karma, but you can obtain forgiveness and grace only by asking with purity of heart. So the Baptists say, "Once saved, always saved." The Pentecostals say, "Oh, you can backslide back to Hell." We Angels say you are both right. For example, if you are "saved," or in other words "awake," started your spiritual walk back home, and you lose your way through "wrong" decisions or directions, all you have to do is ask for deliverance and to be found, and you will be. Then you will ascend.

Those who refuse to cry out or ask even though they are awake will send themselves downward to descension because they haven't truly asked. Every sign, every rest stop, every fill-up station, and every restaurant and hotel has been laid out for you for your destination. You even have a tour guide (Guardian Angel). It is up to you to use it. You see . . . your choice.

*I am confused by the Catholic Church and its ability to say
this is a miracle, and this is not. Where does their power
come from?*

You see, most of the priests, nuns, monks, and clergy of the
Church really have come back to do an "all night cram ses-
sion." In other words, a lot of lives before had not been so
productive, so they choose to come into a very religious
school to learn. Now, do you see things differently? Many of
them who have come in through the Church have been great
teachers—Padre Pio, Mother Teresa, Saint Bernadette. They
choose to come in and teach the clergy and the world. Why
do you think they had miracles and mysticism around them?
Because they were teachers. Now, to finish the question: The
Church gets its power or grant in God because God did start
this school. The Church has made very big decisions that did-
n't get an *A-plus*—kind of like a lab experiment blowing up
and hurting people and matter all over the room. Take for
instance, the Inquisition. Need we say more? Because of some
"bad" or "low" grades, the Church is very careful what they
decide on. This is a good thing. They have learned from "bad
explosions."

*How many dimensions, layers, or rungs on the ladder
are there in Heaven or Hell?*

You see, this changes as your thoughts change. But your mind
is a powerful tool that creates in just the earthly dimensions.
The Spirit creates in all dimensions. For example, a religious
fanatic believes equally in his mind that there are no layers to
Heaven. Just ascension. Now, guess what? That is what he creates for himself. Spiritually, he knows that there have been

layers to go through, and he has gone through several ascensions. So they are both right, and both are being created at the same time. So, where does the Spirit/soul go? Straight home, because they both agree on the highest destination.

If we all serve one God, why then are there so many different religions?

If you are all choosing to serve the same God, and you are all choosing to go home, then why don't you all have the same paths? Have you ever thought that, as humans, you are only ready for certain truths—that, at moments, your perspectives will change? Not everybody is in the same place, spiritually, mentally, emotionally, and physically. Religions are man-made, and many of them contain certain truths; truths, referring to the truths about God and your existence. We cannot say that there is one religion that contains the entire truth. There are certain spiritual truths that cannot be changed or altered. As your lifespan goes on, you'll understand this. You cannot change God's love, nor can you change the direction your soul is going in. No matter what you create, you're always headed back home. Some of you just create certain fear-based "stops" along the way. No matter what direction, no matter how much you drive in a circle, at the end, you return home.

I believe it quotes in the Bible that "God changeth not!" You can't change your origin or the fact that you are a part of the eternal being, which is God. It does not matter what you call this Source or if you even acknowledge this Source; God still is! These are some of the eternal truths. Many religions will reject this one truth because they are a part of the belief system that you are deserving of punishment and damnation. We say this belief is certainly an untruth, and we would encourage you to release this belief if you have "bought in" to this egoic manmade idea. You are deserving of eternity, peace, and love. Your true origin contains all of this.

Manmade religions should be viewed as steps that lead up to a beautiful monument that is your true home. Each step contains a truth that will lead you to the next step, but you have to do the walking! You have to keep your focus on the "monument" or Heaven. There has not been one religion that contains all of the Heavenly truths, and even if there was, we would not refer to it as a religion but as a spiritual body. Some of the organized belief systems that are the closest to the truths are what you refer to as mystics. Mystic beliefs are generally guarded and only shared with those who are open and ready to accept that there are truths in the universe that they belong to and that their humanly mind has not yet been taught.

Why do people have different soul purposes?

Why do people have different colors of underwear? Because you are made in the creation of the one true God, and you are a creator also! As a creator, you will try many different tasks or purposes. You create through experience, and you will have many different lifetimes just like underwear. Do you understand? It's simply because you can and will experience all that each task or purpose has for you. Each purpose has you discovering more of who you are and who God is. For example, in 1629, you decide that you would have the soul purpose of being a servant and working in a household full of people who were dominating and controlling. In that life, acting as the servant, you learned humility and trust. You see? Each and every lifetime, no matter how insignificant you think you were, counts! A purpose is simply the task or job that allows you to discover the real you and God, and maybe if the others are lucky, they will be affected by your purpose and awakening also. It's about being a part of the whole. There is never a time when you do not affect others. You are a part of the "one body," remember?

Why aren't some people intuitive?

First of all, everyone is intuitive, but not everyone uses this ability. The more you begin to "wake up" and realize your true Source, the more you will crave or want to connect with this true Source. The true Source is then viewed as the Mother and Father, and just like a child who is homesick, you will begin to want to speak and see your "parents." As the desire for your parents or God grows, the spiritual senses will present themselves to you for you to use. In this case, you want to "phone home"! All you have to have is the desire, and just like a treasure chest, they will open and dump out all the jewels or talents to bless you with. There is nothing that will ever prevent you from using these talents but you. You have them, and when you are spiritually ready, they will magically appear and begin working for you. Now, we said spiritually ready. This means God's timing and the timing of your soul and Spirit's readiness. Sometimes your mind or your heart or your physical body is not so ready, but don't worry. It will catch up to the rest that is ready.

If we all have a soul contract, then why do some people choose not to follow?

Because they are forgetting their origin, and they are simply running amuck. They are sort of like a toddler who wants to play by his or her own rules and not listen to the parents. However, God is a wonderful parent, and do not worry about not getting back on path because God has been known to allow you to be swallowed by a whale or locked in a prison to set things back in perspective. You have a soul contract that you helped write, and in order for you to come back to your origin, you have to follow your soul's path. God loves you so much that He/She will never let you stray. For many of you, God has to take drastic steps to get through to you and get you back on task. The more you run and push God away, the harder you make it on yourself. God doesn't punish, but He/She will take whatever measure possible to keep you to the soul contract. We Angels know exactly what you have signed up for, and it is our job in creation to keep you on track. We counsel, protect, and guide you back in the direction of your true home.

Why aren't people always happy?

Well, in order to answer this question, we will need to interpret what true happiness really means. Your dictionary defines happiness as the quality of being content; pleasure. True happiness comes from a peaceful soul, and a peaceful soul comes from a relationship and communion with God. When you are in this true relationship, there is nothing on Earth, even a martyrdom of a death, that will steal this from you. People are not happy because they don't remember God and have not tried to build this relationship. Happiness originates from the soul, and it obviously comes from a soul that is content with its creator. When you find your happiness has escaped you, reconnect to the only Source there is. God is always waiting for you and has all the time in the world.

Why are lessons so hard on Earth?

Because you make it that way. It's because you are holding on to the egoic pattern of your mind and the way you think things have to be. If it hurts, it is because you are losing an old pattern of the egoic mind. Something has to die for the new spiritual truth to be born. Each death takes you a step closer to the life that is your Spirit and all the truths the Spirit contains. You think things should be one way, but God knows how things should really be. In this day and age, we would suggest that you let go and let God act because changes are coming quick and fast and not always the way you think they should be. God always knows best, and if you are unsure of this, just ask Him/Her. Life is about letting go and knowing that anything that is true and worth lasting eternity will truly never be lost or disappear. If it's a marriage and it ends, bless it and that Spirit and know that you will be together for eternity. If it's a death, bless the passing and the Spirit and know that they are still around you and with you. If it's a loss of material means, know that God needs you to be free of these earthly ties and that there is more coming to you in many different forms. Allow yourself the acceptance and peace that comes with trusting the Hand of Fate. God always moves the Hand of Fate.

*Are there truly no spouses, or relatives in the
Heavenly realm?*

There is only true, complete existence in the Heavenly realms,
but no such need for "special relationships." You are, of
course, in remembrance of these relationships in Heaven, but
you do not stay in this conscious state. You are in complete
knowing and belonging with the entire Heavenly body, and
this is why in Heaven you finally feel complete. When you are
in the earthly body, you never quite seem to have a feeling of
completeness. Have you ever noticed that? You may feel complete for a while, but if it is based on a person or an earthly
object, and that leaves you, then what? You feel incomplete.
You spend most of your lifetimes feeling incomplete. Why do
you think the Bible refers to the waters of life that never cease
and fill you within? Your "cup runneth over." Is any of this
making sense to you? When you are at full awakening, you
are home and feel complete. When you are in earthly relationships, you are never complete because you are not seeing
your relationship to the entire body.

*What is a soul mate and how do you know when you have
found them?*

A soul mate is a Spirit that you have agreed in your soul contract to meet and learn and walk with in a lifetime. The relationships do not always last because a soul mate is always
created to teach you or give you a spiritual lesson. Sometimes
they are cruel and hurt you. This is an opportunity for you to
learn forgiveness. Sometimes they love you unconditionally.
This is an opportunity for you to learn how to love. Sometimes they die and leave the Earth. This is an opportunity for

you to reach higher to the spiritual realms and connect with the truth of their existence and your existence and God's existence. Each soul mate brings a message and a gift. How will you know them?

You will generally feel a true soul connection and magnetism. You will want them in your life and feel empty and scared when they are not. When you are with them, you seem to know more of whom you are and where you are going. They will energetically carry a piece of you with them, and eventually they will give it back to you in order for you to become whole. A soul mate is essential in helping you find yourself and God. When you and they are in Heaven, both of you agree to this soul exchange. It is imperative that you honor them, forgive them, love them, and release them in order for you to truly make your ascent back home.

Author's Biography

I was born in this lifetime and in this body Taffeny Dawn Hicks on September 5, 1975, at Baptist Hospital in Tennessee. My parents are James Hicks and Peggy Stinson. Upon my arrival, I almost died, but God had other plans. All of my thanks to the doctor who delivered me, because he knew I was corded. He wheeled my mother to the OR, and at eleven o'clock a.m. I was born safely. I believe that I was conceived from the purest love, and I believe that my father's prayers saved my life that day. I suppose I should have known from my entrance into the world and my odd name (a mix-up at the hospital) that life for me would not be very normal. At the age of three, my parents separated, and life as I knew it began to change.

From that point on, with the exception of a few memories, I do not recall most of my childhood. The earliest occurrence of an interaction with a Spirit was at my grandmother's house in Gallatin, Tennessee. It was a dark form, male in its presence. I remember being very scared. My cousin had also seen the outline of the figure that kept appearing to her and me. I suppose, as all children do, we feel fear upon seeing a Spirit, and we try to adjust to what is.

Most of the time we did not tell our parents about our most fearful and powerful experiences. My maternal grandmother, Sadie Clubbs was always an inspiration to my family and me. Most of the time when I would stay with her, and she was busy working, I would hear her talking to someone out loud. When I would go to her and ask who she was talking to, she would tell me that she was talking to God, who is our best friend. She was a pillar of strength and a woman of faith, and never did she ever turn anyone away. She taught me two very important things. She taught me to always tell someone when you love them, because you may never get the chance to say that again on this Earth. The other thing that she taught me is that our church is the Temple of our Soul. We do not have to go to a building or anywhere else on this planet, but right inside of ourselves to meet and talk with God.

My grandmother, Sadie, was also an intuitive; however, she did not speak of it. She would always laugh and say, "I saw it in the cards." I named my child after her, and she guides me often. She still speaks to me, and when I am troubled and down, she lights my path. For her, I am truly thankful. I had more experiences at my other grandparents' farm in New Haven, Kentucky. The house was built in 1790 and is a beautiful, large farmhouse with fifteen rooms and high ceilings. This house has always been very important to my life because not only was I conceived in that house, but I would spend a week to two every summer being with my grandparents on the farm and feeling like I had come home. I suppose not everyone gets to feel all the Angels and light beings at first. For some reason, just as in the farmhouse, all of the lost souls and the darker beings would make their way to the end of the bed and show themselves to me.

As a child, the only remedy I knew for this discomfort would be to hide under the covers and pray earnestly that God would deliver me from their presence. God always did, but I never knew at that age that they were asking me for help. From a very young age around the time *The Exorcist* came out, I knew that somehow I would be involved with deliverance of demons and freeing lost souls into the light. For most of my life, I ran from this conviction. At age thirteen, I began attending a Southern Baptist Church with my friend. Here, I believed that my conviction was because I was lost, and so I became saved.

At this point, the occurrences stopped and my conviction about my life's purpose subsided. It is important to note here that my mother was raised missionary-Baptist, and supposedly I am a 16th Cherokee Indian Nation. My great-grandmother Lucy, Sadie's mother, was a midwife and an herbalist with Cherokee blood. She was also a spiritual intuitive, and yet never spoke much of it either. It is from her that I attribute a lot of my life's work and talents. My father, on the other hand, grew up very strict Catholic and at the age of fourteen, attended Gethsemane Abbey and took his first spiritual sabbatical. Upon my birth, my father insisted I be christened as a Catholic. My mother gave her consent with one exception. She told my father, "We can christen Taffeny in the Catholic Church, but she is not going to be raised Catholic or Baptist. She is going to be raised to choose her own spirituality." No truer words were spoken . . . Thanks, Mom. My mother like my grandmother and great-grandmother has the gift of spiritual intuition, but she shut hers down at a very young age.

One day, my mother was walking with one of her best friends down a country road to her friend's mother's store, when my mother said to her best friend, "Mr. Todd just died." Her best friend replied, "What?" And my mother said, "Didn't you just hear that?" After the two of them arrived at the store a little while later, a local resident came in to report Mr. Todd had just died. My mother, feeling scared of judgment and not understanding her own gifts, shut down for many years. It was not until I was a teenager that she began to open up and truly listen to the voice of God. I suppose also, at this point, I should tell you that I am born one of nine children, three girls and six boys.

My siblings, as are my parents, are just as important to me as any part of my life's experiences, for them I am truly thankful. As far as my coping mechanisms with the dark and the lost souls, I always kept my experiences to myself. Not knowing that my mother and grandmother and great aunts and great-grandmother were intuitive. I felt afraid to speak of what I had experienced. For many years after my baptism, the experiences disappeared and teenage life began, although I never lost an interest in the spiritual realm. When I was fifteen, I bought my first book on Angels by Sophy Burnham titled *A Book of Angels*. Around this period of my life, my mother began speaking with the Angelic realm, mainly Archangel Raphael.

My mother would automatically write, and one day as we sat at the kitchen table, reading what she had been writing, it occurred to me that I wanted to hear the Angels and see them more than anything in this world. I asked my mother that if she could see and hear them, why couldn't I, considering I was her daughter. My mother replied, "Oh, you will in time." It wasn't until after I had my first child at the age of twenty-one that I began to have paranormal experiences again. My husband and I had moved into my mother's house, which I had grown up in, when my son was just four months old.

One morning as I was getting ready for work, I heard a loud voice call my name, and I went across the house to the front door, assuming that it was my father-in-law who had come to babysit my son that day. I found no one there. The voice called my name two more times, and just as I was beginning to get fearful, my father-in-law arrived. Not long after that one afternoon, my husband and son and I were relaxing in the house, and I had another experience. A Spirit came up behind me as I was in the back of the house, and I got so frightened, I ran across the house and jumped on the couch with my husband, whom at this point thought I had lost my mind.

At that moment, I could see in my intuitive mind that it was the Spirit of my aunt who was fulfilling the promise she made me. It is important to note here that my aunt lived with me for several years, and as my mother worked in Tennessee and we lived in Kentucky, she was for the most part my surrogate mother. Eight years before my aunt died, she and I made a pact. We promised one another, that whichever of us that passed over first, we would come back to the other and tell what Heaven was really like. Good old Aunt Dede was fulfilling her promise to me, but scaring me to death at the same time. I had forgotten how stubborn, intense, and determined she could be.

At this point, my husband was afraid I was losing my mind. My marriage probably began to slowly unravel over the next eleven years. The point of surrender that put me on my spiritual path consciously would have to be, when I was pregnant with my second child at age twenty-three and had just begun attending massage therapy school. One of my instructors, Chanin, became my best friend, and she taught me how to clear myself, meditate, and hear Spirit. All I had to do was open my mind and my heart, and trust in God. Then I heard my Spirit Guide, Grandfather, for the first time. He brought the hawk to me as my power animal to give me strength, vision, and awareness in this lifetime. Hawk remains with me to this day, leaving me feathers, calling out to me, flying beside of me as I am driving in my car, and making his presence known at some of the lowest points of my life.

I believe that God is everything, and when we feel we have lost our way or we are about ready to abort our mission, God will take any form to reach us and give us strength and new life. From that point on, many opportunities were given to me from the massage school, one being energy work. In that class, we were offered Reiki initiations, and I felt very called to do the work and take the Rites. I began learning about myself, my past lives, and my soul's purpose, all of which my husband hated and resented. He was raised very strict Pentecostal and everything outside of the box must be of the Devil. For many years while I was growing, I was also trying to prove my worth to my husband—without any great results. This led to many arguments and at one point, the discussion of separation. I could never understand why if Christ said you can tell a tree by the fruit it bears, and I was doing good work that I thought were of God, why he could not open his mind and accept that God is not a Pentecostal form, but all forms to all people.

When my daughter was three, I formed my own business. My partners and I were in business for a couple of years when fate and life circumstances pulled us in different directions. I had to go out on my own. I live in the middle of forty acres and made the decision to build a two-room cabin from which to do my therapy and spiritual counseling sessions. The spiritual counseling sessions began to really take off in 2002. I don't recall my first vision of an Angel; it just seems like they have always been there. There are never moments when I cannot hear them or when I am not aware of their presence. Their teachings and counseling have changed my life and has given me the strength to grow through some very difficult situations. My former husband and I divorced, and the reason for this is that I am going in a direction that he could not go spiritually.

I have learned several lessons with my walk with him, and I am blessed to have had the experience. Here are some of my lessons: We come together with certain souls because we are at a certain place on our path. Sometimes we choose to walk our path with them, and sometimes we come to a place on our path where we must part from them. This does not mean that anyone is wrong, but it means that we are right to follow the soul plan within us. As bittersweet and as difficult as it is, we are all teachers to one another. Only remembering that we are connected eternally and a part of one another is what gives me the strength and courage to move forward on my path. In my heart and in my mind, I believe and know that at the end of the lifetime, the most important thing is that we fulfilled our mission and did the work we were sent down here to do. It is about sacrificing as Christ did for the good of the whole. In my particular case, I suppose my marriage was sacrificed because I had to be what God made me to be.

I have a deep conviction in my heart for my brothers and sisters down here who are struggling to find their way home.

I believe that I am just a vessel and a servant and will go where God sends me. My prayer is that I reflect the love of God and learn to forget my ego. I am a work in progress. I suppose, at this point, you would like to know what I am qualified to do and the services that I have started. I am a board-licensed massage therapist, a certified doula (birth assistant), Reiki Master, and offer saliva and hair testing for holistic treatments. Every other week, I channel a Master Spirit named Ecclesiastics, we call him "E" for short. I channel "E" at our Spirit Group Meetings, which happens to be our church. The Group was formed seven years ago with just me and three other friends. Since then, it has grown to twenty or more. Some would say they are clairaudient or clairsentient or clairvoyant, but I use all of them. I see the Angels, I hear the Angels, and I feel the Angels, along with Spirits and the lost souls of the world.

My children, Tanner and Tiffany, were also born with spiritual talents. My son who is sixteen was born and delivered exactly as I was and has the same gifts that I have. He too feels a call to the lost souls of the world and wants to help mankind. He has a compassionate heart and a strong determination. At one of my lowest points, my son and I had a talk one day. Tanner and I have our special moments, and this means we sit together or he lies in my lap, and we talk to the Angelic Realm for one another.

On this particular day, I was pretty low, and my son said to me with tears in his eyes, "Mommy, I am so glad that I chose you and that you are spiritually made the way that you are." Then, he began sobbing and said, "If I had been born with any other mommy, they would not understand how I was made."

It was at that point that I realized that there was no turning back on my path, because not only for the good of the world, but it was for the very gift of life, my son, that I was made this way. At that point, I realized that God does not make mistakes, and there are no coincidences.

My son sees the lost souls and the Angels and is also an animal communicator. I teach him and my daughter every other week at the children's Spirit group before the adults meet. This group was formed for the children because not only do they have spiritual talents, but I understand what it feels like to be in a world where you don't fit in the box because of how God made you. I work with the children and help enhance their spiritual talents and their relationship with the creator and one another.

Within the year I intend to form an organization for intuitive children and their parents. I want to work with these children to help them understand themselves and their plan, and I want to work with their parents to understand their children and show them the way to also open up. This is a big conviction for me. Tiffany is thirteen, and is one of the most loving Spirits to walk the planet. When Tiffany was conceived, she had a fraternal twin named Tyler. I knew that I had conceived twins and informed the doctor on my first visit, at which they thought, as did my husband, that I had lost my mind. I knew I was carrying a girl and a boy, and I could feel their souls within me. At three months, I miscarried with Tyler, and from that day on, he has never left me. It was not until my divorce that Tyler told me the real reason of his departure.

Tyler said he had to have a mommy and daddy to stay together for his soul path. His spirit stayed with the children and me, and he spoke to us often. He told me that he will come in as soon as I am to find my soul mate on this planet. Well, I have found my soul mate and Tyler has been born to us as promised. I am so blessed. As for Tiffany, at an early age she never saw the darkness, but could only see the Angels and the light. Not to mention the fact that she is a mind reader, so I had to learn to guard my thoughts and block her from my private thoughts. Full of compassion, I believe she is a crystalline and Tanner is an Indigo.

I want to dedicate this book to my aunt Trish, who was my godmother in this lifetime. She died at the age of fifty on July 23, 2005. She was my confidante, my cheerleader, and truly understood my mission and work down here. I had the privilege of helping her battle her cancer, and for that experience, I am forever changed. Her death has given me the strength to become who I am, and my work will always be a tribute to her memory. When she got sick, her motto became "This was never a battle or a struggle, only a journey. Lead me and I will follow." She is with me often, and when I need a firm hand and a strong voice, she is there to guide me.

I am so grateful for my Spirit family and my Angelic family and my earthly family. Without them, I am not sure if I would have arrived at this point. What are some of the missions I was sent down here for? To build a holistic clinic, to write several books, and to reach as many people with the light as possible. When I asked God what my soul purpose was, God simply spoke to me and said, "You are to help people to remember who they are." I hope that at the end of my walk when I meet my Father and Mother in Heaven, they will say to me, "Well done."